Smoky Mountain Tales:

Feuds, Murder & Mayhem

Volume One

Dr. Gail Palmer

"As usual, Dr. Palmer spins a good yarn in the style, and often in the vernacular, of her beloved Appalachian kin folks. Some of the accounts were familiar but others were new to me. All were captivating and entertaining. As the old adage goes, history is a compilation of rumor. However, via scholarly interpretations of the clues she had to go on, she skillfully breathed life into these tales."

Allen R. Coggins,
author and Smoky Mountain tour guide.

"Dr. Gail Palmer has produced a large body of work on the Great Smoky Mountains that includes two books and two DVDs. Her most recent book, "Smoky Mountain Tales, Volume I: Feuds, Murder & Mayhem," shares a native's look at the mountain people, a captivating and entertaining model for communicating local history through storytelling."

East Tennessee Historical Society
2013 Community History Award brochure

COVER PHOTO

Taken by Kathleen Puckett, Nov.16, 2012, 6:05 P.M.,
from a pull-off on Foothills Parkway facing southwest
down Happy Valley toward Chilhowee Dam.

ISBN: 978-0-9823735-4-5: 0-9823735-4-6

DEDICATION

Smoky Mountain Tales: Feuds, Murder & Mayhem, Volume 1, is dedicated to all descendants whose families lived at one time within the boundaries of present-day Great Smoky Mountains National Park, including my mother, Mary Jane (Sparks) Palmer.

Mary Jane (Sparks) Palmer and husband, James Spencer Palmer

Foreword

The stories in this book are based on information found in Park archives and other sources, including books, articles, web sites and court documents. Archival material reviewed includes Park ranger notes and interviews with individuals who lived in the Smoky Mountains before the Park came into being in the 1930s and 1940s. A more complete list of sources is on page 133.

This book is creative non-fiction, stories based on truth but told as fiction. Conversations of characters and thoughts of individuals have been created by the author. Exceptions include testimony gathered from trial testimony, in which case, quotes are sometimes gathered from court records, and interview transcripts.

Using this method of story telling is directed toward presenting the broadest possible word picture of the individuals operating within their own time frame and using their own language. Much of the dialogue is based on the spoken language as heard by the author growing up, mostly in family settings.

The situations in which these individuals find themselves are those reported in interviews and notes found by the author during the research process.

The outcomes experienced by the individuals as presented in these stories follow as much as possible those given within original notes and reports, as well as records of court testimony. Other outcomes are those surmised by the author based on material found as a result of research.

Acknowledgments

So many people have helped create this book. The photography skills of Kathleen Puckett and the graphic skills of Linda Weaver created a beautiful cover. Kathleen added her considerable talents as an observer and writer, especially with the delivery scene in "Devil Child" and the church scene in "One Drop of Blood." Julie Brown, Tremont Institute, added her special talents as an editor to bring out needed changes to clear up confusions of one sort or another, especially in some of the muddled relationships found during research for "Murder in the Foothills of the Smokies." Dr. Susan Jones, former director of Blount County Historical Museum, asked thoughtful questions and offered helpful suggestions, such as giving the story of the Bote Mountain girl the title of "Smoky Mountains Romeo and Juliet." As always, Pam Hindle gave always insightful and enlightened comments, finding humor in comments made by some of the individuals portrayed.

It's always a pleasure to work with each and every one of these individuals. Their comments and suggestions added nuggets of change that enhanced the stories throughout.

Research activities for this work involved visits to the Tennessee State Library and Archives in Nashville, Tenn., and to the Federal Archives in Atlanta, Ga. In both places, the exceptional staff provided knowledgeable assistance and led to the exact materials needed.

Of course, Tim Fisher and his staff at King Family Library, part of Sevier County Library, provided invaluable assistance in tracking down information about individuals located in Sevier County, Tenn. Personnel at Blount County Library, Maryville, Tenn., also provided wonderful assistance, as always.

Earlier, in the midst of doing research for "Cemeteries of the Smokies" as well as for DVDs, "Sacred Places of the Smokies," and "When Mama Was the Doctor: Medicine Women of the Smokies," Annette Hartigan, Park Librarian, always exceeded my expectations for finding information and materials in the National Park Service library at Sugarlands, Tenn.

Other invaluable research sources in East Tennessee include East Tennessee Historical Society in Knoxville and the volumes of material provided at University of Tennessee Library's Great Smoky Mountains Regional Project.

Allen Coggins, author of <u>Place Names of the</u> Smokies and other works, provided review comments that are included on page ii.

All have my thanks and my gratitude. It is their assistance that helped bring this book into reality as well as the willingness of descendants and others to share their knowledge and experiences of life as it was in the Great Smoky Mountains.

Introduction: Whiskey Business

It all started at the beginning of this country with the Scots-Irish settlers. They're credited with bringing what they knew about making whiskey when they migrated to this country. However, it didn't take long for government officials to see whisky as a revenue opportunity. The Washington administration placed an excise tax on whiskey as early as 1791. Farmers in western Pennsylvania immediately saw the new tax as an infringement on their right to change corn into liquid, making it easier to transport and more profitable. So, in 1794, farmers rebelled. The rebellion soon folded and the federal excise tax remained in place until 1817, when it was lifted. Later, in 1862, the federal excise tax came back. Then in 1878, federal managers of the federal excise tax decided to offer a blanket pardon to any moonshine maker. Some accepted, in spite of their continuing to ply their trade.

In 1878, the State of Tennessee passed short-lived legislation that outlawed the manufacturing of whiskey in Tennessee. Until that time, many in the Smokies had built up substantial and legitimate whiskey-making businesses with distillery licenses and official tax stamps on their products. George W. Powell of Chestnut Flats was one such individual who pursued his whiskey-making enterprise whether it was regulated by the state or the federal government. Some of those who continued to make whiskey illegally began hauling a little something "extra" in their wagons as they took apples to market in Maryville or Knoxville from Cades Cove, Chestnut Flats or Cosby. Some had a special place reserved in the local livery stable where anyone could come if they wanted to buy whiskey.

However, the Federal Government's right to regulate the manufacturing of whiskey in the states was decided by a Tennessee Supreme Court decision in 1878 in Tenn. v. Davis. James Davis was a federal revenue officer accused of killing a moonshine operator in self-defense as he tried to arrest the moon-shiner. Davis was declared within his right as a federal agent to use lethal self-defense in the performance of his duty. This case shifted supremacy in moonshine prosecution cases to the federal government and its agents. It pitted moon-shiners against "revenuers" and created a tradition of animosity "between revenuers and moon shiners that would last to the present" (Ellis, 1988).

And so, some whiskey makers continued to ignore the law. They had invested heavily in their businesses and didn't want to give up that revenue source. Those who continued to make untaxed whiskey immediately became outlaws pursued by federal as well as local law enforcement officers. Because of this, they learned to hide their whiskey-making and selling activities. Few people noticed as they hauled sacks of corn and sugar up a hollow, or saw smoke curl up into the mist of a hollow in the evening. Many of those who did notice turned away…these moon-shiners were friends and neighbors, people they knew and whom they were reluctant to turn over to the law. They knew their families, too, and understood the families would be the ones to suffer most if their men lost their livelihood of making whiskey and selling it.

Since they competed with one another, they realized they could sometimes get an edge over a fellow moon-shiner by reporting the location of someone else's still. Others saw moon shining as a way of supplementing their income and ran a line only now and then. Most everyone used some whiskey as part of a remedy occasionally.

Horace Kephart, a writer who lived in the mountains of North Carolina in the early 1900s, described the area of Sugarlands, a community outside Gatlinburg, as being a "country of ill fame, hidden deep in remote gorges, difficult of access, tenanted by a sparse population who preferred to be a law unto themselves. For many a year it had been known on our side as Blockaders' glory, which is the same as saying Moon-shiners' Paradise, and we all believed it to be fitly named." (Some moon-shiners considered themselves "blockaders" because they had to run through a blockade of lawmen in order to deliver their goods. The term may have emerged because of its use during the Civil War when federal ships were denied access to Southern ports. It was true, moon-shiners probably did feel as though they were under siege by the federal government when the 1878 court decision was reached, and later, when the 18th Amendment to the U. S. Constitution created Federal Prohibition.)

It is thought by some that Kephart exaggerated somewhat his descriptions of the area as "Moon-shiners' Paradise," even though the Cosby area of East Tennessee gained fame later as the "Moonshine Capital of the World." Author Gladys Trentham Russell, who grew up in Sugarlands, thought that fewer than 20 percent of mountain families ever participated in making whiskey, although many used liquor as a medicinal or an ingredient they added to their herbal medications.

Moonshine still of the author's Uncle Tige, somewhere in Great Smoky Mountains. This photo shows William Hardy "Tige" Sparks, a brother of Mary Sparks Palmer. Another man is pouring out a sample of their work into a glass. The lid of the still is covered with rocks, in order to hold it down tight. The still is most likely located close to a mountain stream with the cold, clear water necessary for making good whiskey. (Courtesy, Carol Sparks Gregory and Jean Sparks Blevins).

Horace Kephart, well-known author who lived in the Smokies, was outspoken in his support of the creation of a national park in the mountains of East Tennessee and Western North Carolina. He was killed in a car wreck near Bryson City, NC, and is buried in Bryson City Cemetery. A large boulder marks his grave. (Courtesy, NPS).

CONTENTS

Chapter One

The Way I Heard It...

Sometimes, hearing a story from a family member is the only way to learn what happened years ago. The following stories are some that have come from a family member, or come from one then embellished by another. Elements of each are probably true, but it's hard to sort out which is which. That's left to the reader to decide.

"Go West, Young Man, Go West..."
(This quote first appeared in an 1851 Terre Haute Express editorial by John B. L. Soule, but is often said to have come from Horace Greeley, New York Tribune, who used it in an 1865 editorial. The original sentence was "Go West, young man, and grow up with the country," to encourage settlement of the west. It is used here to express advice given to a young man in Tennessee by his grandmother.)

One bright, beautiful spring day in the mountains of East Tennessee in the 1800s, the air felt soft and warm to the skin. Trees were showing new leaves, plants fresh blooms. Honeybees buzzed around flowers, birds chirped as they made their nests.

It was springtime and John was going to meet a girl down by the Little River. John decided to slick down his hair using just a touch of Granny's homemade lard. He dabbed at the creamy white texture with his fingers and rubbed it between the palms of his hands, then rubbed his hands through his mop of blondish brown hair. He patted his hair, the grease having had the desired effect of flattening his hair to his head. He gave his hair one more pat, then hurried toward the door of the cabin.

"Where you going to, son?" the voice of his grandmother floated up to him from the garden as his foot hit the last step leading to the flat, clean-swept yard in front of the cabin. Thunderhead Mountain towered over the Cove to the east toward North Carolina.

"Goin' down to the river, Mamaw," he answered.

"You be kerful now, ya' hear," she hollered back.

He waved to her and crossed the yard in three long strides. He didn't want to be late. He'd told Mary Lou he'd be there afore noon and it was almost that now, according to the angle of the sun. He hurried down the steep mountain path, missing roots and rocks as he loped along. He'd lived in these mountains all his life and knew almost every hollow and valley, every tree and shrub, every kink in Little River as it ran through Tuckaleechee Valley. The river was at its peak now, what with spring rains swelling its boundaries as it ran down the hills toward the flat lands.

He slowed down as he neared the river and began walking. No sense letting her know he'd been in such a gol-danged hurry, he thought.

He reached out and touched a branch as he went by, pulling a green pungent leaf from it. He rubbed the leaf between his fingers and held it up to his nose. He always did like the smell of crushed green leaves in the springtime. His granny knew every plant by name and by its use as a tea or a medicine. It was her mama that taught her when she was just a small girl. Her mama was said to have been Cherokee, but he wasn't sure about that. People just didn't talk too much about that kind of thing.

He slowed down even more, cautious now, placing both palms on the sides of his head and smoothing his hair back. He wondered if she had gotten there first. He peeked around a branch toward the riverbank. The river was roaring now, making it difficult to hear much.

At first he didn't see her, but he came up even with the bush at the side of the path and peered around, then jerked back.

"She's here," he thought. He decided to pretend he hadn't seen her and ambled onto the rocks down to the shoreline, his leather-soled work boots moving quickly over the river-smoothed stones along the riverside. He bent over and picked up several flat stones, sorting through them to find those best suited for skimming across the water. His heart was beating fast and loud and suddenly he felt shy. He'd known her all his life, but suddenly he was at a loss for words.

He stood and placed one stone in his right hand, then pulled his arm back before he flipped the stone forward with a twist of his wrist. It seemed to bounce on the dark water, once, twice, no! Four times!

"Well, John Sparks, you certainly know how to throw those stones around. Never seen no one hit the water four times a-fore." He turned to see Mary Lou walking toward him, blue eyes shining. She stopped and bent over, selecting four flat stones. She placed one in her right hand, taking time to position it just so in the curve of her index finger, then leaned back and gave the stone a toss toward the river. It, too, barely touched the water and seemed to bounce its way across the stream...once, twice...John held his breath...three times!

She laughed and turned toward him.

"Yur not so bad yourself," John said. He began walking toward her. They were alone here on the bank of the river, the rush of its waters the only sound, even his boots made no noise as he walked over the river rock.

Out of the corner of his eye, John noticed a bush at the side of the river moving back and forth. He glanced at other nearby bushes and could see no other movement.

He grabbed Mary Lou's hand and pulled on it until she was between him and the river, then he turned to face the bushes and whatever was coming from that direction. A painter jumped on his Uncle not too long ago as he walked up alongside Anthony Creek on his way to Spence Field and his herding cabin. Tom escaped but not without a few scratches and bites. Course, it could be a bear, too, but usually they weren't anxious to get near people, so he sort of thought it couldn't be a bear.

"John, why did you pull me over here, then turn your back on me?"

John held his hand out toward Mary Lou, motioning for her to be quiet.

"Thought I saw something over there," he said, trying to keep his voice low but not covered up by the sound of the river.

Mary Lou looked around John toward the edge of the riverbank. He pulled a pistol out of his pants pocket and cocked it, pointing it toward the movement.

Just then, the branches moved to the left and the barrel of a shotgun poked out, pointing straight at them.

"Get away from my girl, you no-good skunk," a man shouted as he stepped out of the bushes at the edge of the riverbank and pointed the gun at John.

"Poppa!" the girl screamed. John jumped at the sound. His gun hand jerked and pulled the trigger, firing a round toward the man standing at the edge of the bank.

The man screamed and bent over, reaching down, then he fell to the ground.

Mary Lou ran around John toward her father.

"Oh, lordy, you done killed him!" Mary Lou screamed. John took a step toward them, but Mary Lou looked at him and shouted, "No! Don't you come near him!"

John looked a moment longer toward the figure on the ground, now lifeless, blood oozing out onto the ground.

"I'm sorry," he said, then turned and ran. He had to get back up to the Cove and his granny. She'd know what to do.

He hurried back up the mountain trail and through the Cove to Sparks Lane. He hollered at granny, still in the vegetable and herb patch she kept at the back of the house. She looked up and saw John running toward the house, then taking the steps two at a time up to the porch and into the house. She dropped the basket in which she'd been gathering herbs and ran to the cabin herself.

John was inside, throwing a few clothes into a carpetbag.

"Lord, John, what's a-going on! Looks like the Devil his self is a-chasing' you!"

"Granny, I shot Mary Lou's father, probably killed him. I've got to go now, they'll come after me and hang me, for sure," he yelled.

"Oh, Lord, I guess you do need to go, I know they'd hang you for sure if you stayed here. But where're you going, son?" Granny said. John was her brother's son, but she'd raised him since he was nine after his stepmother threw him into the fireplace and his father brought him to her and her husband, Nate.

"To Californy, I guess," he said. "Don't rightly know where else to go. 'Sides, always heard 'bout people finding gold in Californy…might as well try my luck there, too!"

"Laws amercy, you a gold digger!" she said, her hand up at her mouth. John smiled when she said that. "Might be fun to be a Gold Digger, Mamaw. You'd sure 'nuff like it iffen I was to come home carryin' a sackful of gold on my back!" he laughed.

Granny couldn't help but laugh at that idea, but he was going to be so far away, she thought, and who knows for how long. She might never see him again. She turned and hurried toward the chest where she kept her own clothes and linens and things, rummaged down inside and pulled out a long, wool sock she knitted last winter. She kept her egg money here, money Mr. Gregory paid for whatever eggs or peas or such she took by his store. The sock was heavy. She hardly ever spent any money out of it, usually not until Christmas or when someone needed new shoes or something. She held it in the palm of her hand for a moment, judging its weight, then walked toward John.

"Here, son, you're a-goin' to need this if you're a-goin' all the way to Californy," she stuffed it into his coat pocket.

"Aw, granny, I surely thank ye for that and I'll pay you back, I promise. I'll let you know when I stop somewhere…."

"When you comin' back?"

"Soon as I know I'm not goin' to get hung for killing old man Myers, Granny. Let me know when you hear what they're goin' to do and I'll come back iffen I can."

Granny held her hand up to his face and stroked his cheek. He grabbed her and held on for a few minutes, then let her go and rushed out the front door, down the steps and off through the woods toward Schoolhouse Gap into Tuckaleechee. He knew he could hop a train in Maryville, for sure, maybe even in Tuckaleechee. He knew some fellers workin' down there at Little River Lumber.

Granny stood on the porch a few minutes, watching him go. She waved back to him when he looked over his shoulder, then turned and disappeared into the trees.

Four long years later, Granny wrote to John, telling him to come on home. He'd hopped a train in Townsend and made it all the way across the country to California. One of their kin who'd gone to California had stopped by to tell her they'd seen him and he was doing fine, working in a lumber camp as a cook, then as a muleskinner. They took her letter with them to let him know he could come back.

Months later, there he was, walking up the path as though he'd never left. He was taller and had filled out some, she thought as she watched him make his way toward her.

"Hel-loo," he called, the sound of his voice floating up the hill toward her. She raised her hand and watched as he came into the swept-clean yard in front of the cabin, then strode over to her. She grabbed him and hugged him to her.

"Land sake, John," she said, smiling and laughing as they looked at one another.

"You sure 'nough look good to these tired old eyes," she said.

"Why, what you talkin' 'bout, Granny, you're still a young chicken," he said. "Now, tell me everything…looks like you think I'm not goin' to be hung after all."

"No, no," she smiled. "Mr. Myers just got shot in the foot!" She started laughing, then John did, too. He'd gone all the way to Californy to escape hanging over accidently shooting a man in the foot.

"Well, I'm glad he's OK," John said, "but I'm glad I went out West. It was really something and I'll have to tell you all about it." Something caught his eye as he turned to go into the cabin. A young woman stood in the doorway of the cabin, watching them.

He smiled and nodded toward her.

Granny noticed the two lookin' at one another.

"John, this here's Lizzy Shuler. She's come over from Dry Valley to help me out with the chores. Getting' harder for me to keep up with everythin'. James Shuler's her father and he brung her up here about a month or so ago," Granny said. She motioned for Lizzy to come out onto the porch. She was the oldest girl in her family and it was customary to find a family, usually related, in which she could live and help the family with whatever chores came about.

Lizzy walked over to Granny and John. Her dress went to the top of her high button shoes. Sleeves of her dress went to her wrists and the dress was fastened up to her neck. Lace formed a line from one shoulder to the next. Her clothes looked clean and pressed, the result John was sure of hand washing and pressing with a hearth iron.

"You that Golddigger feller I herred so much talk about?" she said, lookin' up at him, big blue eyes shining out with from a slender heart-shaped face, her skin a light caramel color.

He laughed and shook his head. "Golddigger, is it? Well, shore hate to disappoint you but never did get no chance to dig for no gold. Met a few fellars who did that, though, and they found a few nuggets. They said it was back-breaking work and you had to have enough money to buy supplies and stuff to take with you," John said.

"Well, what did you do if you didn't dig for any gold?" she asked.

"Worked on a mule train hauling logs out of the mountains," John said.

"Do tell," Lizzy said, blue eyes twinkling.

"Come on in, John, and sit down," Granny said. "Lizzy bring John some of that sweet tea you just made and put out the biscuits and some of that ham. You must be starvin'."

John followed his granny into the house and sat at the kitchen table. He couldn't stop watching Lizzy, though, as she moved gracefully across the floor to the icebox and back to the table to pour some tea for him.

He took a sip of tea. "Delicious!" he said. "Sure have missed havin' sweet tea to drink, Mamaw," John said. He looked at Lizzy over the top of the glass as he drank the tea. Losing Mary Lou wasn't so bad, he thought. Seems he'd come home just in time.

A few years later, John and Lizzy were married right there in Granny's cabin, surrounded by the fields and hollows and blue smoke mountains he'd grown up in. They had 12 children, several there in Granny's cabin across from the Oliver cabin and in sight of Thunderhead Mountain.

He was glad to be home.

John and Elizabeth are buried in Salem Baptist Church Cemetery, off Montvale Road in west Maryville, alongside their oldest child, Dewey. He was killed at age 12 when he tried to stop a runaway horse by jumping from the wagon to the back of the horse. He fell and the wagon ran over him.

The rest of John and Elizabeth's children lived to adulthood, including my mother, Mary Jane Sparks, who married my father, James Spencer Palmer. My brother, Jerry, lives in Maryville.

My mother's youngest sibling, Lester Sparks, is in his 90s as this is written. He and his wife, Angela, live in Florida.

John Marion Sparks　　　*Elizabeth Jane Shuler*

*John Marion Sparks and Elizabeth Shuler Sparks
and their three oldest children, (l.to r.) Maybelle,
Margie and Dewey. (Courtesy, Carol Sparks
Gregory and Jean Sparks Blevins).*

32

Mule train on which John Sparks worked while in California. John is thought to be at the very back on the left. He was about 16 years old. (Courtesy, Anna Kay Abbott Morgan).

Here, John stands next to the mule train on which he worked in California. (Courtesy, Anna Kay Abbott Morgan).

Eliza Jane Potter Sparks, wife of
Nathan H. Sparks; grandmother
of John Marion Sparks. (Courtesy,
NPS).

Chapter 2

The Last "Painter" of the Smokies

John Thomas Sparks led the life of a herder. He had a two-story home on the west side of Sparks Lane in Cades Cove and lived there with his family during the winters, but had a cabin on Spence Field across the state line in North Carolina where he stayed during the summers. His father, Nathan Sparks, owned the land and later gave it to Tom. This is a fictional account of what happened to him in his encounter one day with a mountain lion (or "painter" as mountain people called them) and how he died on top of the mountain at Spence Field.

He slung the sack of salt over one shoulder, trying to ease the weight of it as he walked up the trail.

"Durn, got a later start than I planned," he thought, looking up at the trees towerin' overhead, the light already beginning to fade.

Even though he'd been up and down Anthony Creek Trail lo these many years, he knew he'd have to keep his mind on where he put his feet, 'specially with so many rocks and tree roots stickin' out everywhere.

He walked on up the trail, the creek next to him bubbling merrily as it flowed over and splashed onto the rocks and down the mountainside.

He looked with longing at the creek as he passed some of his favorite fishing holes. "Maybe next time," he thought.

He shifted the salt to the other side of his back and tightened his grip on it. He usually carried his shotgun in his right hand, but didn't have it with him this day. Normally, he used it to shoot game, like squirrels or turkeys, whenever his supplies were a little low.

"Nothin' like a good turkey stew," he thought, his mouth watering at the thought. He had some at the cabin on Spence Field left over from last night that he would heat up on the hearth.

"Course, there's probably some fellers up there now who've dropped in since I been down the hill," he thought. "Maybe they'll have it heated up already."

A little further up he knew some of the folks who lived on the other side of the creek. 'Maybe I can stop for a few minutes, just to visit," he thought. "Nah, it's likely be too late," he said to himself. It was already gettin' dark and he was havin' trouble seein' the trail in front of him. Snow from a few days ago still hung on, "hangin' on for more," his Ma said.

He knew this trail as they say, "like the back of his hand," after years of walking up and down it every week or so. He recognized any change immediately. Still, in the dimming light, it was getting harder to see the trail.

"I'll be glad to get to the cabin," he thought. "Tomorrow, I'll go 'round to the licks and dump some of this salt out for all the livestock."

Putting out salt for the animals was just part of his job as a herder, Tom knew. "Gives me a chance to check the herd out, too, see if any are missin'." Mostly, the sheep stayed with the same group they came up with on top of the bald, so it made it fairly easy to see how they were doing when they came to the salt lick. The cattle strayed into the woods, but only a reasonable distance away because of the salt. Most families had herds of 10-20 cattle and maybe 15-20 sheep for their own use. Those heading to Spence Field began driving their stock in Sevierville and Maryville, up Bote Mountain Road. The herders charged $1 or $2 for cattle, a little less for sheep and a little more for horses and mules.

"Might have to cut down another log or two and chop some holes in them to put the salt into," he thought, remembering that some of the logs down now had been there forever and were beginning to break apart, spilling the salt onto the ground.

He always liked hearing the bells on the collars of the lead cattle and sheep sound out as they moved across the balds and through the woods. That was another way he kept track of where the herds were. But when he wanted them to come in, he always yelled out "Hooooo-cow" or "Sue-coooooow!" One or the other would cause them to move his way. Especially if the salt he'd put out earlier was mostly gone.

It was a good life, he thought. Especially staying on the balds about four months from May to September. He looked at the sky through the trees and could see a star or two as they began to come out and fill the velvet blue of the night sky. " 'Course, I won't really get a good look at 'em 'til I get up on top," he thought, then smiled. He truly loved watchin' the stars and the planets move across the sky on a clear night. And this was a clear night. "Moon ought to be up pretty soon," he thought. He welcomed the soft light of the moon as he knew it would light his way up the mountain, but it would blot out some of his star-gazing.

"No way a storm's comin' with that clear sky," he thought. The cattle always scattered whenever a storm came along and he hated trapsin' through the laurel hells after a storm tryin' to find them.

Or, if a bear was after them. That was the worst. 'Bout scares the poor cows out of their udders, he thought, smiling. Really wasn't a laughin' matter when it happened, though. Sometimes the bears were able to corner a cow and take it down. When that happened, he sent word to the Cove and some of the men came up the mountain to hunt the bear. Brought their dogs with 'em to help track it down. Usually didn't take long to find it, either. Although, iffen a bear made it into a doghobble area, the dogs wouldn't follow. No sirree, them dogs won't go into no doghobble hell, Tom thought. It's a plant that's low to the ground with sharp-edged leaves, too low to bother them bears, but it sure nuff tears up the underbelly of them dogs.

"Glad we haven't had many painters," he thought, lookin' 'round him into the darkness of the trees across the creek. Now and again one killed a sheep, even a cow, but not often enough to be a problem. In fact, Tom couldn't remember ever seein' one in these woods. The big cats were too secretive and quiet.

"Except when they scream," he thought, and shuttered. He had heard that sound and it was eerie. There'd been stories about painters in the mountains since the first white settlers come in, 'specially when people first started living in the coves and hollers.

He remembered one story where two painters had jumped on the roof of a cabin one night over in Old Cataluche in the early years, trying to tear it up so's they could get inside, even tried coming down the chimney. The two women inside had been cooking pork and the smell drove the hungry animals to overcome their fear of being around people…and fire, too.

It's said they stayed on that rooftop 'til daylight, then they jumped down and melted into the forest. Scared the daylights out of those two women, he thought.

And he'd heard another story, this one of a woman riding a horse when it was almost dark. A painter had trailed them up the mountain until it finally jumped on the rump of the horse. The horse was so frightened it ran faster than it ever had before, with the woman clinging to its neck. Eventually the horse bucked and kicked until it shook the painter off. "Heard tell that horse ran another mile afore it knew the painter was gone," Tom chuckled.

But the darndest story 'bout painters he'd ever heard was the one about the woman up in Cataluche who'd gone to Little Cataluche to visit her daughter and stayed longer than she'd planned. It was late afternoon when she started walking home. A short distance down the road she thought she heard something in the woods. She turned and didn't see anything, so kept on walking. Further down the trail, she heard a noise again. Her heart almost stopped, but she turned around slowly and there it was, a tawny blond fierce looking painter. It was on the trail, maybe 100 feet away, sniffing where she had walked.

She had no weapons with her and didn't know what to do. Then she realized the big cat was sniffing the trail for her scent. And it was stopping every few feet to examine where she'd stepped.

"Well, iffen it wants somethin' to sniff, I'll give it something to sniff'," she said. She pulled off the shawl wrapped around her shoulders and dropped it in a pile in the middle of the road.

"There. Hope that keeps you busy long enough for me to get on down the road," she thought, hurrying down the path. She turned to look back and the painter was almost where she left the shawl. She turned back to the trail, trying to hurry without causing the painter to start chasin' her. "Lord, Lord, don't know what I'd do iffen it took off runnin' this a-way," she thought. "It would catch me fer sure! Don't know iffen I could climb one of them there trees, even with a painter pushin' up behind me!"

And so, she made her way home, stopping at every bend in the road to drop another piece of clothing.

Tom heard that when she got home, dependin' on who was tellin' the story, she almost didn't have any clothes left. "Durn good thing she got home when she did!" Tom smiled at the thought.

But the men in the house took off after that painter and killed it. Which was too bad, in a way, since there weren't many of those animals left. He kinda liked the idea there was still some wildness in the mountains. Bears were about the only wild ones left now. The Cherokee said wolves left years ago at the first sound of Daniel Foute's bloomery forge in Cades Cove on Forge Creek Road to make iron ore and beat it into shape to make tools.

Tom walked on, shifting the salt bag from one side to the other. He was just about to walk up the last part of the trail before it hit Bote Mountain Road when he heard something. He stopped and turned.

"Helloooo!" he called, then waited to see if he got an answer.

Silence. Not even a night bird calling.

"Odd," he thought, "usually some little squirrel or bird or something movin' around, making a noise of some kind." He waited another moment, then started walking up the trail. As an afterthought, he felt in his pocket for his knife. He pulled the knife out and held it in his hand. It was big and felt solid.

Almost immediately, he heard another sound. "Sounds like someone's walkin' behind me," he thought. He started to turn around to see what it was when a heavy weight landed across his back. Something growled...claws tore through his shirt into his back. He felt the hot breath of something as it tried to take his head into its jaws.

He landed on the ground, trying to push the animal away. Sure wisht I had that shotgun with me, he thought. Somehow he was able to twist enough to see its paw on his shoulder. He raised up with one hand, trying to hold the animal back with the other. He stabbed at the creature once, then again; felt it plunge into something resistant, then soft. He had landed a blow into the animal's shoulder, he felt sure.

The animal screamed in pain, jumped away and ran off into the darkness, its long tail stretched out behind it.

Tom lay on the ground, gasping for breath, trying to see where the animal had gone. He checked his arms to see if everything was still intact. His shirt was torn to ribbons and bloodied, whether with his blood or that of the painter, he didn't know. He gingerly touched the top of his shoulders and his arms, his fingers bloody when he held them out in front of him. Even so, he thought the big cat hadn't come out so lucky.

"Pretty sure I got my knife into him deep," Tom said. He was still gasping for breath, so he lay on the ground and waited a few more minutes. His clothes were a bloody mess but he didn't think the cuts were very deep. He managed to turn over and crawl to the stream. He leaned down over a pool of water at the edge of the stream, cupped water into his hands, and splashed it over his arms, his back and the back of his leg. The cold water stung, but he felt some better.

"Don't think that big cat'll be back my way anytime soon," he thought. "Lord, I hope not!"

After a few more minutes, he stood and picked up the salt, then headed on up the mountain toward the cabin.

When he got to the cabin, he saw smoke coming out of the chimney. He walked to the door and flung it open. Two men were inside. They both jumped to their feet, their hands reaching for pistols inside their belts.

"Good lord, man, you scared us to death. We almost kilt you!" one of them said.

He walked into the room and dropped the bag of salt onto the floor, then slumped to the floor beside it.

"What's happened to you? My God, your shoulder, your back! Blood's all over the place, your shirt, your hands. What happened?"

The two men helped Tom up and over to the bed where he sat down. They pulled his shirt off and began to examine his wounds.

"Not as bad as it looks," one man said. "Got anything we can put on this so it won't get infected?"

Tom pointed to a can sittin' on the countertop in the kitchen. The man picked up the can and opened it. He began to take some salve out and touched it to Tom's wounds. Tom gritted his teeth and tried not to show how much it hurt.

"What happened to you?"

"Well, you fellers ain't a-goin' to believe it, but I tangled with one of the biggest dern cats I done ever seed,"

Tom said. "Oww! Kerful whar you put that stuff…it stings a powerful lot!"

"No, I think we believe you on that…these scratches are not bad but there's one or two here that's purty darn deep. Don't know how you gonna sleep…this is gonna be really sore pretty soon."

They helped put more salve on his shoulder, back and leg where the cat had left scratches. Then they tore up an old sheet and wrapped it around his upper arm and back to keep the salve on. He was lucky his wounds were mostly only surface scratches. He'd be sore a few days but no permanent damage was done, they thought.

A few days later, Tom learned the cat didn't come out of the fight nearly as well as he had. Someone from Fontana, North Carolina, stopped at the cabin. They told Tom they'd found a painter with a deep wound in its left shoulder. The wound had become infected and the painter had nearly starved to death before they killed it. It was said to be the last painter in the Smokies, although Larry Sparks, a descendent of Tom's, talks of seeing footprints of painters across a snow-covered field just outside the Smokies.

> *Tom's encounter with a painter was in 1920. Six years later on July 16, Tom himself was killed. Several different stories have circulated about the killing of Tom Sparks. Here's the fictional version of one.*

Tom was a sociable fellow, always inviting people to visit, or travelers to pitch their tent across from his herder's cabin at Spence Field. Sometimes, he had someone stay in the cabin with him to help with his herding duties.

In the summer of 1926, a young man who was a nephew of a man who lived in Cades Cove, Earl Cameron, was staying at Spence Field and helping Tom out.

One day, Tom noticed his wallet was missing from his shirt pocket. He thought one of the men staying there overnight had taken it and asked about it.

"Hope you fellers didn't take my wallet last night, but it's shore 'nuf missin'."

Tom was stoking the fire then turned and looked at Earl.

"Didn't take no wallet," Earl said.

Earl looked down at his feet and stuck his hands into his overalls.

"Ummm," Tom said. He wasn't often exasperated with Earl, or tried not to let it show. But Earl knew he'd just collected some fees from people he was herding for, and he needed to take that money back to his family in Cades Cove.

"Earl, I don't rightly know if you took my wallet or not," Tom said.

Cameron shook his head. "I don't see why you can't loan me some of that there money. You don't need it all…and, besides, I just need a few dollars so's I kin go down to Murville, maybe buy my mama somethin'."

"Well, you'd better just leave, I guess, 'cause I ain't a-gonna lend you any money," Tom said.

The young man slammed his hand against the door. He grabbed a coat off a wall peg, ran out of the cabin and down the path toward the Cove.

Tom watched him run down the trail toward the Cove and shook his head. "I swear to goodness, hope he's alright. Don't think it's right fer me to loan him any money when I know he can't pay me back. And don't rightly know if he's already taken that money last night. And iffen he wants it that bad, then, I can't trust him to be around here," Tom thought. He turned back into the cabin and began fixing some coffee.

Later that day, he saw someone coming up the trail.

"Dog gone, looks like Earl," said Tom. He watched the young man as he came on up to the cabin.

Buck, his dog, was barking at Earl. "Hush, Buck, it's just Earl," he said to the dog. Tom turned and went back into the cabin. He walked to the fireplace and put another log on the fire. His back was to the door.

Earl walked up to the cabin and opened the door, then stood in the doorway.

"Come on in, Earl," Tom called out.

"Tom," Earl said, his voice soft but clear.

Tom looked up and saw Cameron's silhouette outlined in the doorway. Cameron's arm was stretched out toward Tom. He held a pistol in his hand.

"Ain't right you say I took your money," Earl said. He pulled the hammer on the pistol to cock it and began to squeeze the trigger.

Tom looked at Cameron, then at his Spencer shotgun hanging over the door.

Cameron pulled the trigger and fired the pistol. The gun jumped and fire and smoke came out of the barrel. Tom Sparks fell dead onto the cabin floor.

Some sources say Cameron had gone down to Cades Cove when he left the cabin earlier and borrowed a gun from someone he knew in the Cove. No one thinks Cameron told anyone what he planned to do with the gun. The man later apologized for giving Cameron the gun. Cameron was tried and convicted for killing Tom Sparks. Because the cabin was in North Carolina, he was tried in that state rather than in Tennessee. Some folks say that's the reason he was sentenced to only five years in prison. Tom (March 28, 1859/July, 16, 1926) is buried in Southern Methodist Episcopal Church Cemetery in Cades Cove. He was 67.

John Thomas Sparks is buried at Cades Cove Methodist Church Cemetery. His grave is located close to the church at the backside of the building. (Photo by Gail Palmer).

John Thomas Sparks and his dog, Buck, at Spence Field cabin. (Courtesy, NPS).

Chapter 3

Smoky Mountains Romeo & Juliet

It was a bright, October blue-sky day. Elizabeth (or "Cis" as she was known by her family) drank in the bright colors of the fall day in the Smoky Mountains. She was happy. She was so happy on this day. Sam was coming to get her and tomorrow would be their wedding day.

She spread her arms out and twirled around in the grass, her long skirt billowing out around her ankles until she fell down, giggling.

No one else knew, just she and her fiancé, Sam. They had to be careful no one found out, either.

Specially today. She smiled a secret smile. Sam was coming for her. They had gone over the plan carefully. She had gone to the barn early this morning to feed the chickens and milk the cow, as usual. While there, she'd hidden a satchel under the hay. She'd put a few clothes in the bag, along with a keepsake or two, including an embroidered piece given to her by her mother, along with some biscuits.

She and Sam decided she should wait until just after the midday meal, when she usually went to the barn to collect eggs, so they shouldn't suspect anything until after she and Sam were long gone. She was going to go down to the river's edge to meet Sam where he would be waiting for her with two horses. They'd head out before anyone missed her.

They hoped to make it as far as Bote Mountain, almost to the North Carolina line. Once they were in North Carolina they'd be safe, surely, from her family. Her family (especially her pa) were plum set agin her being with Sam. He'd threatened Sam when he found out Sam had come from North Carolina to see her last spring and again in the summer. She and Sam met at the spring sing held at the church.

Sam was Cherokee and Elizabeth thought he was the most beautiful man she'd ever seen, straight shiny black hair, dark eyes, brown skin. He was sweet and kind, too, and almost shy around her.

She frowned. Her Papaw Luke and her Pa Jesse didn't see Sam the same way she did. They were both of one mind on this and said awful things to her, trying to convince her this wasn't the right thing for her to do.

But she knew in her heart this was what she wanted.

"Pa will come around, he'll change his mind once he gets to know Sam," she thought.

"Cis! Cis! Come here and help me out."

"Coming, Mama," she answered and hurried toward the back of the cabin. Her mother, Tilda, stood next to a huge iron pot, She went to the front and called for her daughter.

She glanced toward the iron wash kettle and saw the bubbling water inside, the log fire underneath blazing in the morning sun. They always tried to wash clothes early before the sun's heat made it unbearably hot, even in the shade of the giant oak tree.

"Here, you stir this a while," Tilda told Cis as she handed the long wooden paddle to her. Her mother began loading the family's clothes into the swirling pot. Someone had to stir the clothes around in the soapy water in order for them to come out clean. Earlier, they had gone to the river to beat these same clothes against the river rocks to knock some of the heavier dirt off.

"What you so happy about, girl?" Tilda asked. She looked at Cis closely. "I swear, I hope it's not that Injun boy you've got on your mind. That's nothin' but trouble, believe you me. And I can't protect you agin what your paw might do if he was to find out you're spending time dawdling around, all calf-eyed about some Injun!"

Her mother almost spat the word "Injun" as she said it. Cis was startled. She knew her pa and papaw were both solid against her interest in Sam, but she didn't know her mama felt the same way.

"Listen, girl, you're abrewin' up a mess of trouble, not just in your own family, but in the whole valley, maybe even past that, if you take up with an Injun boy. There's hard feelings that still linger round here 'bout the dealin's people hereabouts had with Injuns early on," Tilda's bright blue eyes echoed the sky as she looked sharply toward Cis. Her face softened as she touched her daughter's face briefly, then turned away, shaking her head.

"Law, law, I swear, it's hard to understand what's gotten into young'uns these days. Even my own level-headed daughter's goin' dizzy on me," Tilda muttered as she picked up more clothes and tossed them into the washing pot. She worried about Cis, her youngest daughter. She sure enough was head strong and dead set on getting her way in almost anything. She sure hoped her fascination with the young Cherokee boy would be over with quickly.

"Lordy, Lordy," she thought, "sure nuf hope Cis don't get it into her head to take off with him one day. Would be just like her to do that." She shook her head, thinking 'bout what Jesse or even Luke would do in that case. Chase 'em down, sure nuf, and bring Cis back. She looked toward Cis standing by the wash pot. She'd heard the rooster crow six times this morning. That usually foretold a death in the family. And she recollected a white dove peckin' at the window sill last week…it didn't get in the house, but iffen it had, that was another old timey predictor of death in the family. She shook her head and turned around three times where she stood to push away such a thought.

"May the Good Lord keep you from harm," she muttered under her breath as she looked to the blue-sky Heaven up above.

Dinner time came and went. Cis helped with the meal, then went to the barn to feed the chickens. Tilda watched her go. She couldn't seem to shake the uneasiness she'd felt earlier. "Bring back any eggs you find," she hollered toward her daughter's back.

"I will, mama, I will." Cis stopped and turned to look at her mother.

"You know, you're about the best mama I ever heard of," she said, then turned and hurried toward the barn.

Tilda watched Cis as she walked away.

"Wonder what brought that on! Don't know what that girl's thinking from one minute to the next," she thought. Her heart lifted, though, as she thought of the words Cis said to her. It was nice to be well-thought of, even by your own daughter. That afternoon, clouds began moving over the mountains and into the Cove. A welcome breeze came across the valley floor. Tilda was busy in the house, putting her loom up. She was anxious to start weaving cloth for winter clothes.

She lifted her head as she felt the fall breeze move through the house and touch her cheek.

"Where's Cis?" she wondered. "Surely, wouldn't take all this time to pick up some eggs."

She realized Cis might have gone on down to the river. She had been drawn to it, too. She might even be sitting there watching the water flow by.

"Cis! Cis! Where are you?" She listened for a moment, and called out again.

She wiped her hands on her apron, and stepped onto the front porch.

"Where could she be?" she thought. She walked down the steps and began walking to the barn. She peeked around the door of the barn. She walked through the door and called out for Cis. She heard nothing but the cackle of the chickens as they strutted about the barn. Several barn cats eyed her, deciding whether to get up and walk to her, or just stay where they were.

She walked over to the haystack on the barn floor. "These men, they're always so messy," she thought as she looked around at the floor where hay had fallen on the floor in a heap. She moved it back with her foot. "Maybe some mouse or something's been messing around in there, trying to make a nest," she thought.

She moved around the hay, heading to the door at the back of the barn. Once outside, she looked down the hillside toward the river. The clouds moved aside long enough for a shaft of sunlight to hit the river so it sparkled as it moved.

It was such a pretty sight, Tilda decided to walk down to the river, just for a minute.

As she walked closer to the river, she noticed something lying on the grass on the bank. Somehow, it looked familiar to her. A few strides took her to where it lay. She stooped over and picked it up. It was the embroidered piece she'd given Cis. "What in the world is this doing here?" she asked out loud, almost hoping to hear an answer.

She stooped over and examined the ground. Horses had been here, not too long ago. Two, she thought.

Her hand flew to her mouth. "Oh, lord!" she cried. She looked up the trail along the river but she could see no one. The trail led to the road going across into Tuckaleechee Valley, then up Scott Mountain along Schoolhouse Gap Road and then Crib Gap, up to Bote Mountain, then to North Carolina.

North Carolina, where the Cherokee live. Where Sam lives. Where he's taking my daughter!

"Ohhhh," she cried out, then lifted her skirts as she turned and ran back toward the barn, then to the house.

"What should I do?" The men were in the fields on the other side of the river and wouldn't be home 'til dark. She'd just have to hitch up Old Betsy and go try to find them. She didn't want to think about what they might do once she told them she thought Cis had run off with Sam to North Carolina.

Finally, Tilda got a saddle and bridle on the horse and rode off toward the fields, fording the river at a shallow place below the house. It didn't take as long to find them as she'd thought. But Old Betsy had stepped along right smart this time around and they were there before she knew it, looking down at Jesse's and Luke's startled faces.

"She's done done it," Tilda said. She slid down off Betsy and turned to tell them what had happened, that Cis had run off with Sam, sure 'nuf.

Understanding moved across the faces of the men like the shadow of the earth over the moon during an eclipse as she talked, telling them what she'd found at the riverbank. They didn't wait to hear all of it, but dropped their tools and climbed into the wagons.

"Stay here, boys, and finish working this field. We're heading back to the house to pick up a few things to take with us in case we have to go searching in North Carolina for them," Jesse said. "The rest of you boys don't need to come. This is private family business and we'll take care of it ourselves," Jesse told the farm hands as he and Luke rode off.

"I'm goin' to kill that Injun," Luke said. "Soon's I get him in shooting distance, I'm goin' to take a bead on him and drop him with one shot!"

"Pa, we don't know what's happened. Just wait 'til we find 'em, then we can decide what to do about it," Jesse said.

Once at the house, they decided not to take the wagon but to unhitch the horses from the wagon and put saddles on 'em and take off. They might stand a chance of catching them.

They made good time as they rode out of Wear Cove and into Tuckaleechee Valley. Once on Schoolhouse Gap Road, they had to slow to a walk in order to go down the steep trail from Scott Mountain and to rest the horses a bit. Later they stopped in White Oak Sinks and let the horses drink from the pool at the bottom of the falls before they moved on up toward Crib Gap.

It was almost dark by this time. Darkness came early in the mountains. As soon as the sun dipped below the rim of the nearest and tallest mountain, dusk was upon them. In the winter, the temperature dropped several degrees almost immediately. This October evening, the temperature change was more than usual for this time of year, so much so that the men shuddered and put on the jackets in their knapsacks.

It was a dark night for traveling in the mountains. There was no moon overhead to light their way. Still, they were able to pick their way carefully up the steep trail leading to Bote Mountain Road.

"We're gonna' need to dismount and lead the horses, Pa," Jesse told his father. "Unless we want these horses to stumble and break a leg."

Luke grumbled, but knew the truth of what his son said. The two of them dismounted and they walked single file up Crib Gap in almost total darkness.

"We got to keep going, can't stop and let them get over the state line," Jesse said.

"Well, it sure 'nuf looks like some horses have been up the trail the last few hours," Luke said as he straightened and stood up after squatting to run his hands over the trail, tryin' to find any sign of horses moving up the mountain. He brushed off his hands when he stood up. Nothin' there that he could tell.

"What you aiming to do, son, when we catch up with 'em," asked Luke. "You ain't gonna' hurt Cis, are you?"

"Reckon I'll tan her hide pretty good for runnin' away like she did," Jesse said.

"Well, hope you aren't too hard on her. But you know, she'll never forgive you if it's that Cherokee she's with and you hurt him," said.

Jesse gave his father a hard look in the darkness. He'd do whatever he damn well pleased and he'd better not hear a word about it from Pa. It was because of her mama being so namby-pamby with Cis that this had happened. You needed a strong hand to keep a girl like Cis from getting into real trouble. Looks like she's done got into a heap of trouble this day.

"She's going to learn a lesson she won't soon forget," Jesse said. Luke said nothing, but hoped his son wouldn't carry through on his threat. Cis was headstrong sometimes, but always a sweet girl. She'd just met someone very different from herself or anyone else she knew and she was eager to begin her adult life.

"She should've waited," Luke said. He heard no answer from his son, who was a few yards up the trail.

Progress up the dark trail was very slow as they picked their way along.

Soon Jesse stopped, then ducked down behind his horse and walked back to Luke.

He whispered to Luke as he pointed up the trail and to the left.

"I think I see where someone's lit a fire up there," he said.

Luke looked in the direction Jesse pointed and could see light flickering through the trees from several yards further up and to the left.

"That's the way the old road goes, I think," Jesse said. "I figured they'd keep going all the way into North Caroliney."

"We have to get closer," Luke said. "We need to know for sure it's them. Let's leave our horses here. Why don't you go on up and circle around so you'll come up on the other side of them. I'll go on up this way and come at them from this side. We'll have 'em surrounded. Be sure to take your rifle with you."

Luke pulled his rifle from its holder on the saddle. "Hope we don't need these," he said, and then started walking up the trail.

Jesse nodded in the darkness, but took the time to load his rifle. He cocked it, then held it in front of him as he walked along.

When Luke saw that the trail began to turn to the left, he walked straight into the trees so he'd come out on the other side of whoever had the campfire. Jesse was behind him and turned left on the trail and kept on going toward the light of the campfire. Luke watched his son for a few minutes. "Lord, I hope he doesn't do anything to hurt anyone," Luke thought. He'd never seen his son quite as angry as he was now. Luke turned and walked on into the trees.

Jesse walked along the path, placing his feet carefully so he made little noise. As he moved through the trees, he could see two people at the fire but he couldn't tell if it was Cis or not.

He moved closer and began to hear voices. He stopped and listened carefully. Not quite close enough to make them out. He moved on up the trail.

"Sam, I hoped we'd make it on into North Carolina by now." The voice was clear. It was Cis.

Jesse was close to their camp by now. He stepped into the light of their campfire, holding his rifle in front of him. Where was Pa? He thought he'd be here by now.

Cis screamed when she saw him. She was sitting on a blanket on the ground, another blanket around her shoulders. Sam sat on one side of her, his arm around her shoulder. Sam turned toward Jesse and began to stand up. Cis stood first, though, and headed toward her father. Sam grabbed her arm and pulled her back toward him.

"You let go of her, you hear!" Jesse shouted. He moved the rifle until it pointed at Sam.

"It's alright, pa, it's alright! Put the gun down, it's alright," Cis said. She stepped toward her father so she was in front of Sam.

Jesse's rifle went off. The bullet hit Cis square in the chest.

"Pa, you shot me!" she said. Her hand went to her chest as a red stain spread across the front of her dress and she began to fall to her knees. Sam grabbed her hand and tried to keep her from falling.

"You get your hands offen her, you dirty Injun!" Jesse yelled. "You've got my daughter and took her away from me! Look what you made me do!"

Jesse dropped his rifle and stepped toward Cis. He pushed Sam away, and then grabbed Cis to him. Sam turned and saw Luke coming toward him with his rifle pointed in his direction. Luke fired his rifle just as Sam jumped toward the woods. The bullet missed Sam as he ran into the woods.

Luke turned toward Jesse who was on his knees, holding Cis to him. Blood covered the front of Cis's dress. She was already dead.

"Oh, my little Cis," Jesse cried as he rocked back and forth. He stroked her face and her hair. "Come on, Cis, wake up now, come on back to us," Jesse said.

Luke came up behind him and placed his hand on his son's shoulder. He knelt down and put his arms around his son and his granddaughter. One was dead, the other, broken.

They stayed that way for quite a while, crouched in the light of the campfire. Soon the fire began to die down and Luke put some more wood on it.

He touched his son's shoulder and told him he had to put Cis down on the blanket. They needed to bury her there on the mountain.

"We can't never let no one know what happened here tonight, not even ma," Luke said. "It was an accident, but we'd have a hard time proving that. So, we're going to bury her here. I'll start digging the grave. We'll lay her down here on the blanket and wrap her up. Son, why don't you start looking for some rocks we can put on top of the grave mound. Come on, now," Luke said.

They laid Cis down on the blanket and wrapped her up. and then Jesse held her one last time, then covered her face with the quilt he kept rolled up, a rope connecting ends so he could carry it over his back in case he had to spend the night in the open.

Jesse got up first and walked down to the horses. He walked back up the trail, leading the horses, and tied them off in a patch of grass. He pulled the saddles and the packs off and laid them on the ground. He knew they'd be there a while and wanted to give the horses a chance to rest before they started back home. He picked up the shovel and pick they kept in the pack on one of the horses and walked over to where his father sat on the blanket next to Cis's body.

"Help me pick out a spot you think she'd like," he told Luke. He looked at Jesse with glazed eyes, but got to his feet and walked around the clearing with Jesse. It just didn't seem right for a child to die before her parents or grandparents.

Soon they realized the center of the clearing was the right place, surrounded by mountain laurel. It was on the slope of a ridge facing west. The afternoon sun would warm the site, even on the coldest day.

Jesse began digging with the pick, and switched to the shovel. Luke brought whatever stones or rocks he could find and placed them next to the grave. He kept the fire going, too, so Jesse would have some light as he dug.

Soon he placed his hands on the edge of the grave and then pulled himself up. It was about four or five feet deep, about six feet long and three feet wide.

He walked over to the pile of rocks, his hands on his hips. "I think we ought to put a layer of these smaller rocks on the very bottom, then put some leaves and branches on top of that." Luke nodded his agreement. Jesse jumped back down into the opening and took the stones as Luke handed them to him and placed them on the ground of the hole. After the bottom of the grave was covered with stones, Luke began to cut branches and handed them to Jesse. He placed them over the rocks until he was satisfied it was soft and fragrant, the way he wanted it to be.

He climbed back up and went to the blanket where Cis's body was. He picked her up and carried her to the side of the grave where he laid her down, then jumped down inside. He turned to face Luke who picked up the small bundle that was his granddaughter and held it out to

Jesse. He took her in his arms and laid her on top of the laurel branches, then placed some branches of a fir tree over her body.

He jumped up on the side of the opening and stood next to Luke, his hat in his hand. "Let's say a few words, Pa." He looked at his father who broke into sobs. Jesse began. "Thank ye, Lord, for bringing this sweet child into our lives. Forgive us, if you can, for following her and causing this to happen. Take care of her and keep her from harm. "We'll always remember you, Cis. We love you and we're sorry for what we did. Amen."

The two men stood together, lost in their own thoughts, as they said goodbye to the girl they'd laid at their feet. "Amen," Luke whispered.

Jesse began to shovel dirt back into the opening. Soon the dirt was mounded over the top of the grave. They placed stones over the mound, a large stone at the head of the grave, a smaller one at the foot. A makeshift cross of two branches stood at the head of the grave in front of the headstone.

They saddled their horses and rode slowly down the trail toward Wear Cove and home.

And so, Elizabeth "Cis" disappeared and was never found. Her grandfather was thought to have also disappeared around 1835 and no one knew what happened to him. But another source indicates he moved to Missouri over a period of three years, in the late 1840s and early 1850s.

Another story says he left in 1835 or 1836 to help move the Cherokee from Georgia to the west. Some other family members moved to Missouri, then the rest moved there, too, by 1851. It's not known if the scenario in this story is close to the truth of what happened to Elizabeth "Cis." It is known that a grave site was noted on Park maps on Bote Mountain Trail from the 1930s, and a Park ranger said he was told it was the grave of a girl who was running away with her boyfriend and was killed by her father and buried there. A descendent said it was thought the boyfriend was someone who was not approved of by the girl's parents. In this story, the young man was a Cherokee and that met with her parents' disapproval. But it's possible the girl's parents could have been for the Union, while the boy's family could have been Confederate (or, vice versa).

This story was written to give the girl an identity and to let her story be known. It is the Smoky Mountain version of Romeo and Juliet.

Bote Mountain Trail – a possible "hanging tree" said to be near the location of the grave. Local men called the tree "the hanging tree" to scare Cherokee men from coming into the area to court women and girls who lived in this section of the mountains.

Chapter 4

Feud in the Sugarlands

This is a fictionalized version of the Brackins/Newman Feud that occurred in Sugarlands, Tenn., in the early 1900s. The story is based on testimony given by the participants in the trial of Davis Brackins, so the killing of Sam Newman is portrayed here as it is described in court documents. Other information comes from archival sources and from genealogical sources.

Davis Brackins sat on the front porch in his rocking chair and looked across the road toward the tree line. The trees were thick and the leaves looked like a solid wall of darkness in the dusk of evening.

All birdsong had stopped, but he thought he heard something and looked down the road as far as he could see, about a quarter-mile, maybe. It was used as the main road over the Smoky Mountains from Tennessee to North Carolina, so it wasn't unusual for travelers to pass by his cabin, even after dark.

The cabin sat some 40-50 yards above the roadway, and Davis had learned from experience it was better to see someone coming from afar than be surprised. Several people had stopped by the last day or two to ask about things he was going to sell. They'd heard he was planning on moving south to a farm outside Cleveland, Tenn., to join his family who'd already made the move. This might be someone wanting to buy something, he thought.

He worked for Champion Fiber Company, a lumber company that bought land in the Smokies. He was paid to patrol boundaries of the several thousand acres they owned. He was paid quarterly and his last paycheck would be coming in a few weeks. He was looking forward to being out of these mountains. He was 60 years old. Some mighty terrible things had happened over those 60 years, including the death of his own son, Andy, last June. They said it was typhoid that killed him. He wiped his hand across his forehead. His eyes clouded as he thought about Andy. It was tough to lose a son.

He remembered finding that young, red-headed boy, Edd McKinley, frozen to death in the heavy snow of a late storm. That was tough, too. They found out later he had been on his way to his grandmother's place in North Carolina. He and his father weren't getting along and he was running away from his home in Cades Cove. They didn't know who he was for the longest time, and buried him in Sugarlands Cemetery. Bought a new pair of overalls, shirt and socks to bury him in, Brackins remembered.

Another face floated across his vision, that of the young man he himself had killed, Art Newman. It was never far from his consciousness, day or night, it seemed. Brackins shook his head as if to try to wipe the memories and the regrets away.

He looked down the road again and finally made out the figure of a man walking up the hill toward him. He watched, sittin' and rockin' slowly in the semi-darkness. His pistol was inside his haversack hanging from the bedpost in the bedroom. Maybe I should go get it, he thought, but then decided to wait until the man was closer. Besides, the log cabin was small, only about 18x20, less than 400 square feet. "I can reach that pistol in three strides, iffen I have to," he thought.

"Hallooo, the cabin!" he heard the greeting floating up to the cabin. It was the man on the road. It was customary in these parts to let people know when you were coming their way.

"Halloo!" he shouted back. He watched as the man came closer, then recognized him by the way he walked, sort of favored his left side from a logging injury some years ago. It was his brother-in-law, Joseph Whaley, coming up from Greenbrier. Hadn't seen him in a long while, must be 15-20 years, Brackins thought. His wife and Joe's first wife were sisters. Wonder why he's here tonight, Brackins thought.

He stood and raised his hand in greeting, watching as Joe came up the road, then turned up the path leading to the cabin.

Brackins walked toward him, down the steps, then down the path a few more steps.

"Well, shore 'nuff good to see ya," Brackins said as he and Joseph Whaley shook hands. "Lord, it's been 15 or 20 years hadn't it, since we seen each other!"

"Glad to be here," Joseph Whaley said, lookin' around the place and up at the cabin. "Right nice spot you have here," he said.

"Thankee, it's the company's cabin, they let me live here while I'm a-workin'. Come on up and sit a spell," Brackins slapped the man on the back as they turned and walked up the path to the house. Brackins opened the door and Joe walked inside first.

"Sit down here," Brackins said, pulling out one of the chairs around the kitchen table. "Was just about to fix sumthin' to eat." He pulled two bowls out of a pie safe and placed them on the table. The pie safe was his Mama's and it was used to keep pies in a place safe from flies. He used it to store his dishes, what few he had. He turned toward the stove, selected a small log, opened the stove box and put the wood inside, then stoked the fire a bit.

"Got some stew here…won't take long to get 'er warmed up," he said. He lifted the lid of a pot on the woodstove then stirred it with a spoon. "Nah, won't take long."

He turned toward the fireplace at one end of the cabin and added some logs to it, stoking it up. Then he lit an oil lantern on the table. The light flickered and sputtered a moment, casting eerie shadows around the room, then settled into a steady flame.

"There," he said. "That should take the gloom off'en this place."

He sat down in the chair facing his visitor.

"Well, how you been?" he asked. "What brings you this a-way?"

Whaley paused, then said, "Well, everyone's doing purt-near good," he offered. "Been workin' for the lumber folks down at Greenbrier and headed over to Little River Logging Company where I'm gonna' work the next few days. Got to be there tomorree. Heard you was gettin' ready to move out, thought I'd stop and ask about your job, if'n anyone's done got it or not."

"No, no one else has got it yet, I reckon, but sure will be glad to put a good word in for you."

The two men chatted a while, Brackins catching up on news of his kin.

The two men ate and talked a while longer, then decided to go to bed. Tomorrow would come and Joe had to get started walking early if he wanted to make it to his job on time. It was some eight-10 miles away.

"Since I only got the one bed here, you're more than welcome to take the wall side of the bed, iffen you like, and I'll take the other side. Make yurself to home," Brackins said.

Whaley went to the side of the room where the bed was and took off his overalls, then laid down on the side of the bed closest to the wall in his long johns and socks and pulled the blanket over himself. Brackins came in after checking the stove and fireplace and turning down the lantern. He took off his work pants and shirt, leaving his long johns on, then lay down on his side of the bed, and pulled the quilt up over him. Soon, both were asleep.

It wasn't long before the thump of heavy boots on the porch sounded in the night.

"What in tarnation?" Brackins asked. He got up out of bed, pulled his britches on over his long johns and walked to the door in his stocking feet.

"Who's there?" he shouted.

"Just me and a couple of the boys," he heard someone say, then what sounded like someone whisperin' and snickerin'. The voice sounded familiar. Then he realized who it was...Sam Newman, the man whose 22-year-old brother he'd killed a few years before. The Newmans lived just down the road from Brackins.

Reluctantly, he unlatched the door and held it cracked open just a bit as they tried to push their way inside. He'd heard Sam had said he was goin' to kill him to get even for him killing Sam's brother, Arthur. "Maybe they'll get tired of hasselin' me and go somewhere's else tonight," Brackins thought. In his heart he knew that wasn't likely, not after he'd asked Squire I. L. Maples to talk to Sam, see if he wouldn't make peace between 'em. Squire Maples talked to Sam about it, but he would have none of it. Brackins knew if they kept coming to his house, trying to kill him, he'd have no choice but to kill them.

"Tires me out a-tryin' to deal with these fellers," Brackins thought.

Finally, he held the door open and they trooped in. Amos Cole, 26, came in first. He was known for making whiskey, selling it and drinking it, too. And he was on a workhouse warrant right now, meaning he'd skipped out while on a work detail. He had a bottle in his hand and took a swig from it, then wiped the back of his hand across his mouth.

On his heels were the Newman brothers, Sam and Tom, 16. Tom was playing a French harp and Amos was dancing around to the tune being played.

"Why you so agin whiskey?" Amos abruptly asked Brackins.

"I'm not agin it," Brackins answered. He lit the lantern and placed it on the table.

"You're the one done shot his brother, Art, ain't you?" Amos said, pointing to Sam.

Brackins couldn't deny it. He had killed Art, Tom's brother, Arthur Bunt Newman, about four years ago, but a jury acquitted him. Bunt had blamed him for the death of his father, Walter Newman. Walter and the rest of his family thought Brackins had reported a still Walter had in the woods. He was found guilt of running a still and the judge told him he could either serve time in jail or he could enlist in the Army. He chose enlisting and was shipped out. He was killed in Europe.

"Don't mention that," Brackins said. "It's a thing of the past." He turned from them and walked toward the bed side of the room.

Someone shoved him forward, then jumped on his back. They fell toward the bed, but landed on the floor. Whaley was still in bed but didn't move or say anything. Brackins wondered briefly how Whaley could be asleep with all this racket a-going on.

He didn't wonder long 'bout Whaley 'cause Cole was on top of him, beatin' him about his head. Brackins was face down on the floor. His gun was still in his haversack on the bedpost.

"I've got to get a-holdt of that gun," Brackins thought, desperate now. He knew for sure they meant to kill him this night to make up for his killing their brother, Bunt, and causing their father, Walter, to be killed in the war.

He twisted round so one hand was free, grunting with the effort. He touched the bag with his fingers, grabbed it and somehow pulled the pistol out with his right hand. All the while they were hitting him with their fists. It was Amos Cole, Sam and Tom, too, for all Brackins knew. He moved his body, lifting his shoulders enough to move the gun underneath his body and over his left arm, then fired the gun at whoever was on his back.

The roar of the 32-20 Colt revolver rang through the cabin. It was a deafening sound and split the still night air in two. The man on top of him let go, then crawled onto the bed. Slowly, Brackins got up offen the floor and looked around. Everyone else was gone. Must of scattered at the sound of the gun, he thought.

"Sure glad all it took was one shot," Brackins mumbled. He put the pistol back in the haversack and pulled on his shoes.

Blood was all over the floor and the bed and spattered over the wall. It was a mess. He'd have to clean it up but he realized Whaley had disappeared.

"Reckon I'd better see where Whaley went to," Brackins said, walking into the kitchen. He wasn't there. Evidently, he'd jumped out of bed when the fight began, grabbed his clothes and went out the kitchen door. Brackins went outside to see if he could find Joe.

"Hey, Joe, you out here? Need to know you're all right," he hollered.

Whaley answered back. "I'm out here, near the spring.," he yelled. It was south of the house. Brackins walked toward Whaley, but looked back toward the house. He saw someone coming out the door and then heading down the road northwest toward the Newmans' house. "Looks like Amos," Brackins thought.

Brackins and Joe stood near the spring and talked for a while.

"Didn't have nothin' to fight with so figured I'd better get out of the way," Whaley said.

Brackins nodded. Didn't blame him for not wantin' to get in the middle of somethin' like that.

"Someone's goin' to be comin' soon, I reckon," Brackins said. He knew Deputy Trentham lived close by and that's probably who Amos went to see. "Why don't you go back inside with me to wait?"

Whaley shook his head. "Nah, don't want to go back in there, don't want to get involved," he said. "Guess I'd better head on out."

"Well, don't blame you," Brackins said. He told Whaley that Sam Newman was shot and killed in the fracus that just took place inside the cabin. He asked him if he'd tell his sons what had happened when he got to Little River Lumber and that he wanted them to meet him in Gatlinburg, to make bond for him. "Be glad to do that," Joe said. He looked down the trail. He could see a light comin' toward them.

"Well, better get goin'," Whaley said. He turned down Brackins' offer of a lantern. "Got a flashlight," he said, then turned and headed away from the light. Later, he tried to find Brackins' sons, but they heard about what had happened before he saw them and were on their way to Gatlinburg.

Brackins' neighbor, Deputy Caleb Trentham, came up the trail and went into the cabin. He found the dead man lying on the bed, his knees on the floor, his body on the bed.

He noticed blood on the floor and on the bed. There was glass in the fireplace from a bottle. Brackins later told him that Amos had thrown the bottle in there the night before.

The next day, Davis Brackins went with Jim Carr and Jim McCarter to Squire I. L. Maples, where they had a preliminary trial. Brackins gave bond, then went to see Dr. Montgomery, the doctor at Elkmont, who treated him for a broken rib.

At the trial, James Carr, Deputy Sheriff, Sevierville, said he'd examined Sam Newman at the scene.

"He was in overalls and there was a hole in them as big as two fingers. There was powder burns on his clothes and the hole was black. There was a shot in his chest left of center in line with his nipples," Carr said.

"The ball come out back an inch to left of center and was two inches higher."

The jury found Brackins guilty, but the Supreme Court of Tennessee reversed that decision and ordered a new trial. The court said the evidence presented by both the state and the defense showed Brackins was not guilty of voluntary manslaughter. Sam Newman knew Brackins was leaving the area and probably thought this would be the last chance he'd have to exact revenge on him for killing his brother four years before.

Davis Brackins was found not guilty and released. He left Sugarlands and moved to the farm he and his family had bought earlier in Cleveland, Tenn., north of Chattanooga. They had moved there several months before.

Brackins was born Oct. 22, 1854, and died July 18, 1939, son of Andrew and Demerius Ramlin Brackins. He married Josephine Cole, daughter of James N. and Mary L. Parton Cole. Brackins and his wife are buried in Macedonia Baptist Church Cemetery, Cleveland, Tenn.

Arthur Bunt Newman was about 18 years old when he was killed. Samuel Newman, his brother, was about 20. They were sons of William M. Newman and Martha Cole.

Brackins home was just below the Goober Farm (used to be a peanut farm, but became the Chimney's Picnic area). Brackins family had already moved to Cleveland, Tenn., so he stayed at the caretaker log cabin at Grassy Patch near Alum Cave. Aaron Huskey built this cabin in 1914 for the caretaker to use when making his boundary inspections. Later, after Davis Brackins left, his nephew, Lewis McCarter, got the job. The Newsmans stayed in Sugarlands and the Gatlinburg area. They sold their land to the State for the Park.

Sugarlands Cemetery (or Burton Ogle Cemetery) is located about two miles down Sugarlands Trail from U.S. Highway 441. Edd McKinley, the 12-year-old red-haired boy found frozen to death in the Park by Davis Brackins, is buried here. The Newman brothers, Arthur and Sam, may be buried here. No markers have been located here with their names inscribed. (Photo by Gail Palmer)

Chapter 5

Miracle in Catalooch

Mama Matt orta' be here soon, Mary thought. She rubbed her hand across her stomach, then stood and walked to the fireplace. She stoked the wood a bit, one hand holding her back. "I'll be glad when this little one gets here. It's takin' a awful long time…it's hurtin an awful lot and them pains is comin' along mighty quick," she said to her husband, Conner.

"She'll be along right soon, I 'spect," he said. "She's as anxious to see this one as you are." He walked to the window and looked across the porch and the yard toward the path that led up the hill to the cabin. It was a beautiful spring day. Leaves on the trees were unfurling. Soon, dogwoods would be in bloom.

"That there's a wonderous sight," he thought. Just then, he noticed movement on the trail.

"Honey, yor mama's done here, so's Papaw Hoyle," he said. "I'll go down and hep 'em up the rest of the way." He opened the door and started across the yard, then opened the gate.

"Howdy, Mamaw, Papaw, glad to see ya! Come on in," he said, hurrying down the path and taking the bundle that Mamaw Matt carried. She carried a stout walkin' stick in the other hand and used it to help push her way on up the steep hill.

Just then, two little girls came runnin' from behind the house, pigtails flying, faces shinin'.

"Mamaw, mamaw, did ya come to see us?" Martha, the oldest asked.

"Why, yes, child, I come to see you. How pretty you look, and you, too, Carrie!"

Both girls giggled, delighted at the attention they were getting from their grandmother, Martha "Matt" Noland.

"Hi, mama," Mary called from the doorway. She held to the frame of the door with one hand and steadied herself with the other hand holding her side.

Mama Matt walked across the swept-clean yard and up the steps. The whole yard was enclosed in a rail-pen, with lumber leaning against other lumber pieces so that one supported the other, forming a zig-zag pattern.

Mama Matt was always just a little anxious 'bout tendin' to a delivery, especially iffen it was her own daughter, as it was now. Mary'd always had a pretty easy time of it, though, no problems through four deliveries.

The two girls, Martha, 12, and Carrie, 10, were both hangin' on to one of Mama Matt's hands, Martha on one side and Carrie on the other. Mama Matt didn't come very often, so they cherished her visits whenever she did.

All three landed on the porch just as Mary turned to go back inside the house. She walked to the rocking chair by the hearth and sat down. The chair was padded with quilts and blankets.

"Land's sake, child, you need to go on and lay down on that there bed in the other room so's I can take a look and see how far 'long you are right now," Mama Matt said. She directed Mary's husband, Conner, to begin boiling some water. He handed her bundle back to her and turned to the cabinet against the wall and pulled out a large pot. He moved the handle on the pump connected to the sink up and down until water streamed into the pot. After it was full, he lifted it and took it to the woodstove and placed it on one of the hot pads.

"Water's on now, Granny Matt," Conner said.

"Thankee, son, bring me some towels when you can," she said, then turned and followed her daughter into the bedroom and watched as she sat on the side of the bed.

"Here, let me help you swing yor legs up and get you settled so you'll be comfortable," Matt said.

Martha and Carrie had followed their mother and grandmother and stood in the doorway of the room.

Martha twisted her pigtail and retied the bow. Carrie looked at the floor and swung one sandled foot back and forth.

"Mama, are you sick? You gonna' be alright?"

"Yes, honey, yes, I'm gonna' be fine. Mama Matt is right here with me and everything's gonna' be fine. Now, you girls need to go on outside and find somethin' to do to stay out of the way while Mama Matt gets ready."

"What's she gonna' do, Mama?"

"Why, child, I'm gettin' ready to catch me a rabbit," she said. She smoothed strands of Martha's hair back behind her ear.

"A rabbit! Oh, granny, you can't catch a rabbit in here! They're outside," Carrie cried, her blue eyes big with excitement at the very idea of catching a rabbit inside the house.

"Why, yes, you're right. You're such a smart girl, Carrie! So, you two need to go on outside and watch to see when the rabbit's comin'. Then you can come in and tell us," Mama Matt said. "Give me a hug first, a'fore you run outside."

The girls crowded against Mama Matt and hugged her, taking in the powder scent they always associated with her, sometimes it was the scent of summer roses, other times, a fragrance of lavendar.

"Yes, go on, girls," their mother said.

They waved bye to their mother and ran across the room and out the door to the front yard, eager to try to be the first one to spot the rabbit that Mama Matt wanted to ketch.

At first, Martha and Carrie circled around the yard, peering into any holes evident in the row of hedges and plants that lined the outside of the rail fence surrounding the yard.

"That's a road for the rabbits," Martha said, knowingly. As the older of the two, she always felt she should know more than Carrie and always took any chance to let Carrie know that.

Carrie looked at each pathway she could find, but no rabbits were evident. They even wondered out to their Mama's garden and went up and down the rows between the beans and tomatos and cabbages. Their mother even had a row of herbs and another of cotton. One row was of tobacco. They had helped their mother take some of the tobacco and hang it in the barn to dry, then twist it into pieces a few inches long. Later, they knew both their mother and grandmother took some of the tobacco to smoke in their pipes, those long-handled pipes that they hid under their aprons and took out only when they thought no one was looking.

Carrie grabbed a plant that had a long stem. She broke it off, then held it to her mouth and blew out, then in.

"Look, Martha," Carrie said, "I'm smokin', just like Mama and Mamaw!"

"Carrie Jane, you put that pipe stem down right now. It's agin the Bible for you to smoke tobaccee," Martha admonished.

Carrie lost interested in the pipe stem and threw it to the ground. Surely, there was something else they could do.

"I don't think any rabbits are comin', do you?" Carrie asked Martha. "Let's go to the wood pile! We can chop some wood! That'll really make Mama and Mamaw happy!"

"Yeah, let's do that," Martha agreed.

They headed toward the stump used as a chopping block.

"Here, I'm the oldest, so I'll do the choppin'," Martha said. She picked up the axe and hefted it in her hands. She had chopped wood before. Her father had showed her how to do it, so she felt pretty confident. Heck, it's easy, she thought to herself.

"Let's get some of these smaller logs and made 'em shorter so they'll fit into the stove," Martha said. She laid the ax on top of the choppin' block and started pulling smaller logs out of the pile on the edge of the yard.

Carrie started picking up logs and the two of them took their stack and put it down next to the chopping block.

"Carrie, pick up a log and put it on the block. After I chop one piece off, you push the log so it's on the block and I can chop another piece off."

Carrie nodded. She picked up a log about as big around as her fist and about four feet long. She placed it on top of the chopping block. She stood on one side of the block and held the log down so it wouldn't bounce off the block when Martha hit it with the ax. Then Carrie pushed the log further onto the block for Martha to chop again until the entire piece of wood had been chopped into four pieces, small enough to fit inside the woodstove.

Martha felt the wood of the ax handle. It was smooth to the touch. She lifted it and felt its heft. She moved her hands to clasp the handle at the bottom end, then lifted it over her head and swung it straight down so that the blade went easily through the wood, efficiently separating the log into two pieces.

She and Carrie developed a rhythm, she lifting and swinging downward, Carrie holding, then sliding the remaining piece further onto the block.

Carrie held the small round log with both hands. Even though she wasn't very tall, she leaned over so that she could hold the wood securely on the block.

Martha paused and leaned the ax against the block while she lifted her arm and wiped the sleeve of her dress across her face. It was only May, but the wood chopping made it hot. She glanced at the pile of wood pieces lying next to the block, all about six or so inches long. She smiled, pleased with herself. "This is way better than keepin' watch for an old rabbit," she thought.

"Carrie, push that piece on across the block and I'll chop this one and I think maybe we'll have enough," Martha said.

Carrie nodded, then pushed the piece of wood toward the middle of the block. Just then, Martha swung the ax down. Carrie's hands were still holding the log down on the block. The blade of the ax sliced through three of her fingers, chopping the tips off. They fell to the ground.

Carrie screamed! She grabbed her hand and ran toward the house, blood streaming down her arm and off her elbow. For just an instant, Martha didn't know what had happened.

"Carrie, Carrie, wait, what happened?" She ran after her sister and up the steps into the house. They burst through the door and into the room where Papaw and Mamaw were sitting. Their mama was lying down in the next room.

Mama Matt stood and grabbed Carrie who was standing in front of her, tears streaming down her face, her right hand clutched tightly in her left. Martha stood behind Carrie and kept saying over and over, "Carrie, I'm so sorry, I didn't mean it! I'm so sorry!"

Papaw Hoyle saw what had happened and yelled out to the boys around the side of the house.

"Boys, hurry and pick up those finger stumps around the choppin' block afore the chickens eat 'em and bring 'em in here, quick!"

The two boys ran to the block and began searching for the fingertips that had been sliced from Carrie's right hand.

"I found 'em, Pa," Tom, the oldest boy, yelled. He stood and raced to the porch, his bare feet slapping on the smooth hard surface of the dirt yard. He held them out in front of him as he ran.

"Lord, boy, don't drop 'em! Just bring 'em here, quick," Pa said. He held a piece of cloth out and Tom placed the three bloody tips onto the cloth.

"Here, Matt, they're all here. Where do you want 'em?" Pa said.

Mama Matt looked at the cloth. "Those were sliced off really slick, got straight edges," she said. "I'm gonna' put 'em back where they were before. Go get some a that shine, we're gonna' have to give her some for the pain. And it's gonna' get worse here in a minute."

He went to the shed outside where he kept his moonshine. It also served as part of the family medicine supplies. Mama Matt had Carrie sit down in the rocker.

"Marthee, I'm a-gonna' have to clean her fingers and it's gonna hurt somethin' awful, so I'm gonna need you to hold onto her and try to keep her still." She turned and took the bottle of whiskey and a glass from her husband.

"She's a-gonna need a lot of this stuff," Mama Matt said as she poured the amber liquid almost to the top. "Bring me some honey and lemon, too, we gotta make it so she can drink it." She prepared the whiskey, then took it to Carrie, who was still crying but not as loudly now. Martha stood next to her with her arm around her.

"Here, take a sip of this, honey, it'll make you feel better."

She held the glass to the girl's mouth and Carrie took one sip, then another. Soon, she'd drunk almost half the whiskey in the glass. She still held her hand tightly, but her tears began to stop and her head began to nod.

"Paw, kin you bring me some of that there turpentine? I think I've got some brown sugar I kin use. Let me look in my bag, I'm a-gonna need some clean white twine."

"Paw, while you're gettin' the turpentine, kin you bring me a board, too? One that's long and as wide as her hand…I'm gonna' have to tie it to that so's she won't move it around and it kin heal."

He came back into the room in a few minutes and held a board out to Matt and placed a can of turpentine on the floor.

"Yes, that'll do, that'll do nicely. Now, I've got to thread this twine into this needle and we'll probably need your help to hold her still while I sew these fingers back on for her."

Matt turned to the young girl, sitting peacefully in the rocker now, her eyes closed. She still clutched one hand with the other. Matt touched her hands and held them for a moment, then began to clean each finger carefully. Carrie groaned but seemed to be asleep. Finally, Matt was satisfied the fingers and tips were as clean as she could make them.

She placed Carrie's hand on top of the board, palm side down. She wrapped a clean white cloth around the hand and the board so that it supported the hand. The fingers were loose and Matt picked them up one at a time.

"Be sure to hold her arm down. Here, Pa, maybe you better do that. Marthee, you go to the stove and bring back a bowl of warm water. I'm gonna need some more soon."

Mama Matt picked up her needle and thread and began to make small incisions in one finger then another, one tip at a time, until she had attached them all back to their original position.

She sat back and surveyed her work. "There, now iffen those tips grow back to the fingers, I think she might keep those tips and be able to use 'em."

She patted the girl's face and woke her enough so that she could drink some more of the whiskey toddy. Her head nodded forward and her eyes closed.

"Paw, lift her up and put her on that bed over there. Put the coverlid over her and make sure she stays warm. Marthee, you can sit with her and if she wakes up, see if you can't get her to take a few more sips of this here medicine."

"Mama! Mama! The baby's comin'," Mary yelled from the bedroom.

"Lord-a-mercy, child, hold on, I'm a-comin'," Matt said. She hurried into the bedroom and examined her daughter. Yes, the baby's comin' and fast. Don't think we'll have to wait very long, she thought. Sure 'nough the baby's head appeared, then the rest of the baby slid out into the towel Matt held ready to catch him.

"It's a boy, Mary, what's his name?" Matt asked.

"Henry's his name," Mary said. Matt cleaned him and wrapped him in a clean towel, then handed him to his mother.

They were sure to remember this date, May 12, 1915.

When Carrie was older, she went to see Dr. Goldman Young of Asheville. He noticed one of her fingers was crooked asked how it happened. When she told him, he wrote an article about the event and it was published in a medical journal. The doctor said Granny Matt was ahead of her time. It wasn't until the 1990s that a successful reattachment was accomplished in a regular surgical setting in this country. After delivering the baby, Granny Matt stayed several days and did whatever needed doing. Back then, it was thought the woman needed to stay in bed 10 days or more after giving birth because it took that long for her bones to go back into place.

Aunt Martha "Granny Matt" Noland
North Carolina midwife

Carrie Noland - As she grew up, she learned to play guitar, banjo and piano. She sewed quits and did whatever she needed to do.

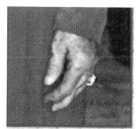

Carrie's hand many years after the miracle surgery performed by her Granny Matt.

Chapter 6

A Gift of Great Price

This is the Story of Tsali (or Charlie) and his wife, Nan'yehi (nan yay hee or Nancy, One who is with the Spirit People).

Historically, the Smoky Mountains have been a place of movement of people from the east crossing over into the western frontier and with one group replacing another. A clear example of such displacement occurred in May of 1838 when all Cherokee were forced by the U. S. government to give up their land in North Carolina, Tennessee, South Carolina and Georgia and move west of the Mississippi River into Indian Territory. The Cherokee appealed to the courts and won their case in the U. S. Supreme Court. However, President Andrew Jackson refused to accept their decision. Since he had control of the troops, the Supreme Court could not enforce their ruling, and the displacement of native peoples began.

Some Cherokee moved before 1838, but most did not. General Winfield Scott came into the area with 7,000 troops to force Cherokee out of their lands. Some 16,000 Cherokee were taken from their homes to "holding pens" until the move west. Many lost their lives in the stockades due to the terrible conditions there. For the rest, the move west meant walking under armed escort across Tennessee and across the Mississippi River into Arkansas and Oklahoma. Gen. Scott ordered that horses or wagons be supplied to those too sick or unable to walk. Even so, this event became known as the Trail of Tears because of the estimated 4,000 Cherokee who lost their lives either in the stockages or along the way. A lingering sadness draped like fog over the Cherokee when they left their beloved Smoky Mountains.

However, some of the Cherokee in North Carolina refused to leave. This is the story of one such family, that of Tsali (Charlie) and his wife, Nan'yehi (Nancy,) and how their eventual resistance helped create a place for Cherokee to remain in their homeland in North Carolina.

Tsali came from Coosawattee Town and earlier in his life was known as a follower of the teachings of Tenskwatawa, brother of Tecumseh and the Shawnee Prophet. Tenskwatawa generated a traditional and religious revival among native tribes. His works are said by some to have inspired the Cherokee Ghost Dance movement, which increased the influence of Shawnee leader, Tecumseh. It was Tecumseh who advocated the joining together of all tribes, to abandon acculturation, and to take up arms against the Americans.

Tsali was considered a traditionalist Cherokee prophet and was asked to speak at the Cherokee National Conference where he spoke in favor of an alliance with Tecumseh. A Cherokee called "The Ridge" (Major Ridge) rejected Tecumseh and his ideas at the conference. Ridge even threatened to kill Tecumseh if he set foot in the Cherokee Nation. Legend has it that Tecumseh promised to bring the rath of the Great Spirit on the earth by stomping his foot on the ground. About the time he arrived back in his home after the council, the 1812 Madrid earthquake struck. Some weeks after that, Tsali spoke to the Council and inspired everyone present, so much so, they were ready to vote in favor of following Tecumseh.. After this, Major Ridge attacked everything Tsali said. It was then that Tsali's followers attacked The Ridge, who was saved only by the intervention of a friend.

Such defiance of Tsali by Major Ridge caused him to lose favor with the other Council members who had been about to vote in favor of supporting Tecumseh's war, but who changed their votes.

In anger at Major Ridge and his defiance, Tsali foretold of a great apocalypse for the Cherokee Nation sometime in the future. "The only safe haven will be the Smoky Mountains of western North Carolina," he told Council members. No apocalypse came at that time, but the Council voted not to support the Americans against the British in the War of 1812.

Many years later, he and his family realized the reality of such an apocalypse as Tsali had prophesized was near when U. S. President Andrew Jackson defied the U. S. Supreme Court by going through with his plans to force removal of the Cherokee from the southeastern United States west to lands in Arkansas and Oklahoma.

Nan'yehi, Tsali's wife, was the matron of their family group consisting of Nan'yehi, Tsali, their three sons and their families and Nan'yehi's brother, Lowney and his family. They lived quietly on a small group of farms near the mouth of the Nantahala River, which flows into Little Tennessee River near Bryson City, NC. Tsali still believed in the teachings of Tecumseh that called for the principle people to return to their native ways and that was the way they lived. Tsali and his family's home was physically outside the boundaries of the Cherokee Nation in the Snowbird Mountains. And, they lived outside the cultural boundaries of much of the rest of the Cherokee, who had taken up the "white man's way" late during the 1700s. Tsali's family and the 1,000 or so Cherokee living at Quallatown, NC, were among those Cherokee considered to be "traditionalists."

Following is a fact-based fictional account of the story of Tsali and might really have happened.

Nan'yehi worked at her loom, listening to her brother, Lowney, as he talked to her husband, Tsali. They sat at the table in front of the fireplace in their cabin in the Snowbird Mountains of western North Carolina. He told Tsali about the white people's army of 7,000 who were rounding up all Cherokee and placing them in stockades.

"They mean to take all Cherokee west, to the land where the setting sun bends down to touch the earth," he said. He used his hands to form the round ball of the sun as it bent down over the land. Although he and the rest of the family spoke English, this night he spoke in their native Cherokee language. It was an important time for their family and he felt it should be told in their native tongue in order to convey the gravity of the situation.

"I fear this will be the apocalypse the spirits showed me all those years ago," Tsali said.

Nancy worked quietly at the loom, flicking a picking stick from one side of the loom to the other. She was making a blanket with a double weave design. She had to use the loom to make something this wide, instead of hand weaving or finger weaving. She liked to weave in the evenings in front of the fire. "It's so relaxing," she thought.

But the news she heard her brother relating to her husband was anything but relaxing. It made her think of another similar prophecy about the Cherokee people, one that told about Nancy Ward, Beloved Woman of their tribe, who died in 1824. Beloved Woman or Ghigau (Ghee gah oo) was the highest honor for a Cherokee woman. She had a voice and a vote in the General Council, leader of the Woman's Council, preparer and server of the ceremonial Black Drink, peace negotiator and the right to save a prisoner condemned to death.

"I had a vision," she had said, "I see a great line of our people marching on foot. Mothers with babies in their arms, fathers with small children on their backs, grandmothers and grandfathers with large bundles on their backs. They were marching west and the Unaka (white soldiers) were behind them. They left a trail of corpses of the weak and the sick who couldn't survive the journey." It is said about 4,000 Cherokee lost their lives along the 800-mile trek westward.

Nancy sat at her loom working quietly. She would remind Tsali of the vision of that other Nancy more than ten years ago. The journey of which her brother spoke must be the journey of which that other Nan'yehi spoke. She was known to have visions that came true. This vision's time has come, Nancy thought.

She stood and walked to the table and sat down. In the Cherokee Nation, men and women were equal, although they divided labor and responsibilities. Women could earn the title of War Woman and sit in councils as equals. Kinship followed the mother with children growing up in the mother's house. Women owned the houses and furnishings and could divorce their husband by placing his belongings outside the house. Women took care of the children and the house, including cultivating the fields. Women owned the land. Men helped some with household chores like sewing but spent most of their time hunting. However, the culture of the European immigrants had a powerful influence on the native peoples and by the 1820s, many Cherokee began living in family groups in log cabins along the streams and rivers rather than in the typical towns of the Cherokee. Tsali and Nancy shared their family farm with their sons and their families.

As Nancy listened, she felt she must remind them of Nancy Ward's vision.

"My husband, my brother," she began, her voice low but compelling. Both looked to her as she began.

"This was foretold by Beloved Woman Nancy Ward," Nancy said and she repeated the story of Nancy Ward's vision. "We must recognize that what she said is coming to pass now. We must prepare ourselves for this journey or we will be among those who will fall and be left along the way."

Both men paused in the smoking of their pipes. They looked at Nancy then looked into the fire. They both nodded slowly. What she said was true, they knew, but it was a hard thing to hear. They and their people had been in this land for as long as they or any of their people could remember. These mountains belonged to them.

Nancy sat at the table with her husband and her brother. She reached under her apron and pulled out a long-stemmed pipe. Then she drew out a small pouch of tobacco. She thought of the days she'd spent planting the tobacoo, harvesting and drying it. She watched as she dropped a pinch of the plant into the pipe bowl. She stood and walked to the fire and, taking a pair of tongs from the hearth tools hanging on one side of the fireplace, she picked up a still-smoldering ember and held it to the bowl of her pipe. She placed the stem into her mouth and took a deep breath, then blew out a stream of smoke. She nodded, satisfied, and dropped the ember back into the fire, turned and sat down at the table once more.

All three were silent, breathing in the smoke from their pipes, then releasing it into the air of the cabin.

"What you say is true, O Nan'yehi," Tsali said. "Yet, we live outside the Cherokee Nation. They are the ones who made the treaty with the whites that allow them to be moved from the mountains. We did not make such a treaty. We own our land. We follow our traditional ways. We should not be sent away. Some Cherokee must stay here to tend to the mountains and the animals and the waters, as our forefathers and mothers did."

Nan'yehi and Lowney nodded solemnly.

"And, too," Lowney said, "we are few against many. They say they have 7,000 mounted warriors. We are old. We are farmers. We have few warriors."

Again, the other two nodded slowly, accepting what was said. They all sat for a long time, smoking together.

"I fear this is the apocalypse come to pass that I spoke of in earlier times. We should ask the spirits to guide us," Tsali said. Again, solemn nods of agreement from Lowney and Nan'yehi.

"If we ask the spirits to guide us, we should be ready to do whatever they ask," Nan'yehi said. "And we should ask ourselves 'are we ready to do whatever they ask?'"

Tsali and Lowney looked at each other, then at Nan'yehi, who was sitting between them, still smoking her pipe and looking down.

Tsali said, "You are right, Nan'yehi, we must search our hearts and know that we are ready to do whatever is asked. When we go to the river tomorrow morning, we will know if we are ready. If that is true, then we must be vigilant in our watch for the signs and have whatever we need to act on them."

"Lowney, we must gather all our family here tomorrow. Go to them and bring them here. Tell them to prepare for a long journey, so if that is our answer, we are ready. If that is not our destiny, we will know by tomorrow and will be ready for that, too."

They sat for a while longer, smoking together. Lowney stood up and walked out the door. He knocked the ashes out of his pipe against the post on the porch and put it into his pocket. He didn't say goodbye for he knew he would be with them tomorrow.

Tsali stood next and walked outside. He stood on the porch and looked at the stars in the sky, then walked behind the cabin to the outhouse, still smoking his pipe.

Nan'yehi stood, then walked to the fireplace, knocked the tobacco embers out of her pipe, then placed the pipe underneath her apron into its pouch.

She looked around the room at the cabin they had built and in which they had raised a family together. She hoped to remember it as she saw it tonight. She knew things would never be the same after tomorrow.

She sighed and walked into the bedroom.

Early the next day, as was their custom, Tsali awoke first and went to the river. Nan-yihee went next after Tsali returned and began the fire in the fireplace.

Later, Lowney came and again they gathered at the table in front of the fire. They smoked their pipes and drank chicory.

Tsali cleared his throat and began to speak.

"I had a dream last night," he began. "I saw the principle people remaining in the mountains and carrying on the traditions and wisdom of our ancestors."

He paused and drew more smoke into his lungs.

"It is decided, then," Nan'yehi said softly.

Tsali nodded. "And so it shall be," he said.

"And so it shall be," Lowney and Nancy echoed.

The three of them began to lay their plans and prepare for the days ahead. They were fortunate to have time to plan...they heard that many of their people had been forced to leave their homes without warning.

After their plans were made, Lowney brought the sons and daughters-in-law to the cabin. They all gathered round and listened as Lowney told them about the soliders and the forced move of their people to the west. Nancy relayed the vision of Beloved Woman Nancy Ward in which such a move was foretold more than 10 years ago.

Finally, Tsali himself spoke and told them of his dream of the principal people remaining in these mountains and carrying on their traditions.

Most of the family members listened quietly. The younger men wanted to fight the soliders, but listened to Tsali and Nan'yehi as they counseled that they had no choice against such numbers.

"The spirits will show the way to accomplish this in spite of the numbers against us," Tsali said.

"We must watch for the signs and be ready to act on them. If we act before it is time, we will be knocked down and no one will be able to remain."

Nancy spoke up. "So. This is what we must do to prepare. Prepare as for a long journey, bundle enough food for many months, pack cooking items, food, tools for firewood and building shelters. All of these things we must have with us," she said.

She assigned something for each of the families to do as part of the necessary preparation for the time when the soldiers came for them.

"We must be ready for that day when the Unaka come to our door. We must have everything ready at hand to pick up and take with us."

"Should we take weapons with us?" one of the sons asked.

"Our tomahawks and knives will serve as our weapons, should we need them," Tsali answered.

Each of the three families left the cabin and began immediately to prepare food, tools, fire starters, clothing and blankets. If they went on the long journey, it would take them into wintertime when little food or shelter would be available along the way. And they would be without their animals and their weapons.

Within a few days, each family stood in readiness.

And so, they went about their usual daily chores as they awaited the coming of the troops.

One day before the sun came up, the knock on the door sounded.

"On order of the President of the United States of America, Andrew Jackson, Brigadier General Winfield Scott hereby orders you to ready yourselves to vacate this property in exchange for other property in the west. You will be provided with food and shelter. Pack only the belongings you can carry with you," the trooper instructed. "We will return for you tomorrow morning at this same time and you will leave whether you are ready or not."

Tsali and Nancy stood on their porch and watched the mounted troops riding down the trail away from the cabin.

"What now, old woman?" Tsali asked of Nancy.

"We do as we said we would, prepare for the journey and watch for signs of the spirits," Nancy said.

Lowney came by soon after the troops left and they asked him to take news of the troopers' visit to the rest of their family.

"Tell them to come here when the sun goes down today. We'll all stay together this night and will be here to meet them at dawn," Nancy said.

Tsali and Nancy lay in their bed, listening to the sounds of their families as they settled down for the night. They lay close as they had since they married.

"Our journey together may end soon, wife," Tsali said.

Nancy looked into his eyes and drew her fingers down his face.

"Yes, it may," she said. "It has been a long and fruitful one. I thank the Great Spirit for allowing us to be together. I pray we are able to do as we're asked and that we survive."

Tsali paused for a long moment. "We may not make it to the mountains ourselves," he said. "Unless we go to the magic lake in the mountains…and we may not go there together."

"You are right, my husband. I trust the Great Spirit to lead each of us down our destined path and I pray that they are one and the same. If not, I trust we will meet on the shores of magic lake for our journey in the spirit world."

Tsali kissed his wife and held her tight. They both fell asleep and slept until dawn.

Four soldiers came soon after dawn to escort them to Bushnell stockade down the Little Tennessee River from Tsali's cabin. The family gathered on the front porch, each holding their bundles in their arms or on their backs. There were 12 people in the small group, five men, seven women and a few children. Second Lieutenant Andrew Jackson Smith and three men led the family away from their home. Smith was the only one on horseback.

Tsali and Nancy took their first steps toward their westward trek from the porch to the walkway in front of the cabin, then through the fence and down the trail toward the small community of Bushnell. As soon as they were out of sight, several white men rushed onto their property and began to pick out whatever they wanted. Soon they left and hurried to the next vacated Cherokee home to loot it as well.

That first night, Tsali and his band were to spend the night at a camp prepared by Lt. Smith and his men at the home of Burton Welch near the junction of the Tuckaseegee and the Little Tennessee rivers. After they'd eaten some of the supplies they brought with them, Nancy spoke to each of the other women and instructed them to conceal knives and tomahawks in their clothing. "We must be ready for whatever comes," she told them.

The next day, they walked along the river and came to the mouth of Paine's Branch, opposite Tuskseegee Creek in the Little Tennessee River.

It was here that Nancy stumbled on the riverstones. She stopped to rub her foot and to adjust her mocassin to make sure it was not loose. One of the soldiers walking behind them prodded her with his bayonet.

"Hurry along, old woman, don't keep us waiting," he said.

Tsali saw what the soldier did to his beloved wife.

"They may move us many miles to the west but they will not treat my wife in such an undignified way," he thought. Anger churned through his system, but he did not show his anger to the troops.

Instead he turned to the others in his group and spoke in his native language. "My family, they cannot understand what I am saying," he paused, smiled and chuckled as though telling a joke. "They will not treat our beloved Nan'yihe in such a manner. That they would do so is a sign from the spirits that it is time for us to act. We will walk to the next turn in the trail. There I will trip and fall and complain of my ankle. When the soldiers stop, leap upon them and take their guns. Then, we'll escape into the hills."

He looked at Nancy and nodded. She nodded back. They continued to walk along the river trail, readying them selves for the action they must take.

They walked for several minutes along the path following the river. They searched ahead for the next turn in their path. It represented their turn toward freedom and escape into the hills.

"I see it ahead," Tsali said, again speaking in his native tongue. The others nodded, their eyes focused on the point in the path ahead where it disappeared to the right as it turned. Two of the men were to pull the mounted trooper to the ground, while the other three were to overpower the other soldiers, disarming them and knocking them down. They would take their weapons, tie them up and leave them, then cross the river and move into the hills to a cave they knew well at the base of one of the tallest mountains in the Smokies. They had the element of surprise in their favor, but no guns. It was a dangerous move but they felt it was the right move to make.

Tsali led his small family group further down the trail to the bend. As he made the turn, he stepped toward a rock, stumbled, then fell to the ground and grabbed his ankle, crying out in pain.

The women in the group rushed to him, while the men hung back and all four troops escorting them, Lt. Smith on horseback, the others walking behind them, turned toward Tsali and moved through the family to where he lay on the ground. As they walked through the family, Lowney jumped on the last man and brought him down to the ground. The others followed suit, but as they did so, the troops fired their weapons and two of them fell dead. They grabbed the lieutenant's jacket and tried to pull him off the horse. One man hit him in the head with a tomahawk, but the lieutenant held to his horse and rode away down the trail.

Tsali and his men worked quickly to urge their family across the river at a low place close by, then move toward the trail that would take them into the hills to their safe place.

The young men were jubilant at their success. Tsali, Nan-yihe and Lowney were more sober. They knew that the deaths of the soldiers would bring more soldiers to hunt them down. It was not what they had wanted nor what they had expected would happen.

"We must trust this will lead to the fulfillment of your dream," Nan-yihe said.

Tsali nodded. They could only hope that their actions would lead to some of their people being able to stay here.

"I fear it means we will not be among those who will stay," Tsali said. He walked ahead, lookling for the hidden pathway that would take them to their hiding place.

Meanwhile, after the escape of Tsali and his family, General Scott soon became convinced his soldiers couldn't recapture Tsali. The General decided it wasn't worth using his troops for the time and effort it would take to bring Tsali and his band in.

And, so, a bargain was struck.

Col. William Thomas was a white who had been adopted by the Cherokee who, as an adult, became a champion for the Cherokee people. He bought land in western North Carolina and held it in his name until the Cherokee were allowed to own land in their own right. He was appointed a chief of the Cherokee and was trusted as one of them.

"Col. Thomas, I look to you to find Tsali and his band and bring them to justice for the killings of the soldiers," Scott said. "In fact, if you will find them and bring them in to be arrested, in exchange, I'll contact the people in Washington and ask that all Cherokee who've not yet been removed be allowed to remain."

Col. Thomas closed his eyes for a moment, thanking the Great Spirit. It was what they had hoped would happen, some way, some how. But at what a horrible price, he thought. To lose Tsali and his sons!

Col. Thomas opened his eyes and cleared his throat.

"A most generous offer, General," Thomas said.

"In all honesty, it solves two problems, one for me and one for the country," Scott said. "I'll be relieved of using my troops and my time dealing with Tsali and his capture will solve the so-called 'Indian problem' by allowing the small group of Cherokee who've managed to elude the removal to remain."

The General offered Thomas a cigar, then took one himself and began to smoke it.

"Do you know where Tsali is?"

"No, they say he's hidden well enough that he won't ever be found. I think I can find someone who knows where to look. The Cherokee of Oconoluftee will have reason to want to see Tsali captured if it means they can remain in the Smokies. I will talk to him, Utsala (Lichen). His followers number about 1,000," Thomas said.

"Fine, that sounds fine. Report back to me as soon as you've talked with him. Believe me, Colonel, this is the only way any of your people have a chance of staying in North Carolina without fear of being captured and shipped west," Scott said.

Thomas rose and the two men shook hands.

Thomas immediately went to Oconoluftee and talked with Utsala who agreed to the General's terms. Thomas relayed his answer to Scott. Tsali's fate was sealed. He, Thomas, would go into the hills to find Tsali. The General offered to supply him an escort for his visit, but Thomas wanted to go alone.

Thomas' horse picked his way carefully along the trail leading up into the highest part of the Smokies until they reached a point where Thomas dismounted and began to walk with his horse further up the trail.

"Ho, friend," a quiet voice said, coming from behind a large chestnut tree along the trail.

Thomas stopped and looked in the direction of the voice, but saw no one.

"Ho, friend," responded Thomas. He knew it was Tsali. Just then, Tsali stepped from behind the tree and grasped Thomas' forearm with his hand. They stood for a moment, face-to-face.

"Will, it's good to see you. So glad you decided to drop by," Tsali said. He looked at his friend with a twinkle in his eyes. "Come, let's go to the place where we're staying. I know Nan'yehi and the others would want to see you…and to hear your news."

Thomas looked at Tsali with narrowed eyes.

"You do have news, do you not?" Tsali said. He turned to look at his friend as they walked up the trail.

"Yes, yes, I do," Thomas said.

"Wait until we're at our camp so everyone can hear what you have to say," Tsali said.

Thomas took a deep breath. He knew the news he carried would be greeted with much mixed emotion. The loss of Tsali and his sons would be a dreadful blow to Nan'yehi and to the rest of his family, as well as many Cherokee. But what they stood to gain in exchange was the stuff of dreams they'd had for some time now, the chance to remain in their beloved Smoky Mountains.

The trail went up and to the right. As they moved around the bend, they came to a wall of mountain laurel plants that looked impassable. Tsali walked straight to the middle of the thicket and pushed a branch to one side and held it until Thomas and his horse moved past it and into a "tunnel" formed by a canopy of laurel branches intertwined overhead.

The path and the laurel thicket led around the mountain and ended at the opening of a large cave created by a stone overhang that extended some 100 feet across. He could see that the cave extended at least that far into the mountain.

"A spring is at the back of the cave," Tsali said, pointing into the darker area at the back of the cave. "There's a hole in the ceiling, too, so any smoke from a fire will go out far above us. Plenty of room for horses is on the other side of the cave and a grazing area. This cave connects with another that leads to another opening several miles from here, a perfect escape route."

Thomas nodded. "I'd heard of this place all my life, but never been here until now. Perfect hiding place," Thomas said.

Tsali nodded, pulling on his pipe and exhaling the smoke so that it seemed to swirl around his turbaned head. Turbans became fashionable for Cherokee men when Sequoyah wore them in the 1820s and was still a favorite for Tsali, especially in colder weather.

"Ah, here she comes," Thomas said, and held his arms out to Nan-yehi. They hugged and stepped back to look at one another.

"You look well, my sister," Thomas said, using the customary greeting for someone in the same clan.

"As do you, my brother," Nan'yehi replied. "Come, let's go in, sit and have something to drink." She led the way as Thomas and Tsali followed. They had created a Council House inside the cave, with a fire in the middle of the round building, surrounded by benches. As they walked in, others followed, until all of their

118

family was present. Soon, Nan-yehi and the other women moved about the group, offering each a cup of hot herbal tea, a drink prepared especially for such gatherings.

After all had been served, Tsali stood to address the gathering. "My brothers and sisters, we have the honor of having Chief William Thomas with us today," Tsali said, nodding toward Thomas, who nodded to the group.

"In light of our recent escape, I'm sure he has come here to deliver a message from Unaka Scott. Let us hear what he has to say, so we can each take it into our hearts and know where our future lies," Tsali said and sat down.

Thomas stood and walked to the center of the room. He looked around at all who were there, at Tsali, Nan'yehi and their family, Lowney and his family. The group seemed relaxed, even joyful, some smiling slightly, some talking to their neighbor. "Doesn't look like a group expecting bad news," thought Thomas.

He cleared his throat, then began to speak.

"I bring greetings from Unaka Chief Scott," Thomas began. "He has said he will allow any Cherokee who has not yet been rounded up to remain in their homeland."

"Ho!" A loud cry of approval rose from the sons of Tsali and some of the other members of the family.

Tsali didn't join in the celebrations but motioned with his long-stemmed pipe for Thomas to continue.

"What does he want in exchange?"

"You're right, brother, he does want something in exchange. He is convinced his troops cannot find you and bring you in, but justice must be served. You and your sons must pay for the killing of the two soldiers escorting you."

The inside of the Council House became silent as the Tsali family absorbed what Thomas had said. A breeze came into the house stirring up the embers of the fire so they flamed upward for a moment, casting tall shadows on the surrounding walls, then fell back.

"So...they think we killed the soldiers," Tsali said.

"Yes."

"Even though we were armed only with knives and tomahawks and the soldiers were shot."

"Yes."

"Ahh," Tsali said.

"So, Tsali and our sons will die so Unaka Scott can save himself from dealing with this dilemma," Nan'yehi said.

"So our people will be free to stay here, my love, and so my vision can come true," Tsali said as he turned to face his wife. "It seems we must each take a different path until we meet at magic lake in the mountain. There we will be reunited and continue on the same path together." Tsali held Nan'yehi's hand. "Think of it! You and our daughters-in-law and our grandchildren will stay here and make a life in our beloved mountains. One part of the prophecies made, those of Beloved Woman Nancy Ward, have come true. This is the time for the second half of that vision shown to us in my dream to come true, as well."

Nan'yehi's eyes glistened but she nodded her head. She knew Tsali was right. Each party had to bring something to the table in order to have a contract. The exchange offered cost a high price, but it would be a way for their family and their tribe to remain in the Smoky Mountains, to keep the old ways and the old wisdom alive in this world. It would be worth it in the years to come for their family.

"It is the path I must follow," Tsali said to Nan'yehi, his voice low and solemn.

Nan'yehi took a deep breath and nodded again. She must accept the way he had chosen. In her heart, she knew it was the right path for him and for their people.

Tsali stood and grasped Thomas' forearm. "Thank you, my brother, for bringing this to us. Return to Unaka Scott and tell him we accept. One thing, though, I will not be brought in by Unaka troops. This must be something that is accomplished by following our own ways and by our own people."

"So, you want Cherokee warriors to have credit for bringing you in."

Tsali smiled. Thomas understood what he wanted and why.

"Yes, I will tell Scott you accept, but that you will give up only to Cherokee warriors."

"Talk with Utsala (Lichen) of the Oconoluftee Cherokee. Explain to him what this means for our people, for his and for mine. Ask him to do this difficult thing for all our peoples. Then come to me and let me know if this is acceptable to Unaka Scott. I will give you a message to deliver to Utsala to arrange a meeting between the two of us."

Col. Thomas walked to the Council House doorway, then toward the edge of the cave, where a young man held his horse by its reins. He accepted the reins and walked toward the opening in the laurel thicket that would take him back to the trail.

He felt relieved Tsali had accepted Scott's offer. He felt sure Scott would allow Utsala's troops to take over the difficult task of capturing Tsali and bringing him to justice. After all, it would not seem as though Tsali's death was at the hands of Scott, but his own people. And he hoped Utsala would accept the task given him by Tsali. Losing Tsali would be a terrible loss for Nan'yehi and the rest of their family. The alternative of Tsali being tracked down by the General's troops and shot down was even worse. At least, this allowed Tsali to be in control of his own destiny and be able to give a gift of great price to his people now and forever.

A few days later, Thomas retraced his steps into the mountains to see Tsali once again to relay Scott's acceptance of Tsali's agreement.

This time it was Nan'yehi who met him on the trail. She held her hand up, palm forward, in greeting. It was a more formal greeting than she had used before. It was a way of reinforcing that this was to be a very solemn occasion.

"Brother, it is well to see you," Nan'yehi said in her native Cherokee.

"And it is well for me, too," responded Thomas.
They turned and began to walk up the trail. Thomas held the reins of his horse and it followed behind them.

"So. Is it well with Unaka Scott?" Nan'yehi asked.
"Yes, it is well. He accepted Tsali's terms. I am to ask Tsali how he wants this to be, and Utsala's role. Then I am to convey that to Utsala, and later Scott."

They continued to walk up the trail. The laurel thicket was so dense Thomas couldn't tell where the entrance was to the thicket until Nan'yehi turned toward it. He and his horse followed her to the opening at the cave.

No one was there to greet them.

"Everyone is in the Council House," Nan'yehi said.

A young man came to Thomas to take his horse for him. Thomas followed Nan'yehi into the Council House. The place was packed. Thomas noticed that members of Tsali's family were seated on the benches in the front. The other benches held many more people than Thomas had seen the time before.

"There must be at least 100 or more people here," Thomas thought. He was amazed.

Those present watched as he followed Nan'yehi to the front where Tsali sat in the middle of one of the benches.

Nan'yehi motioned for him to sit next to Tsala, and she sat next to him.

Soon everyone became quiet.

It was time for the Black Drink, a special potion prepared by Nan'yehi and the other women, for use in this sober ceremony.

Nan'yehi stood. She turned and faced the people, then stretched out her arms and looked up to the ceiling. She began to sing a song to the Great Spirit, asking that they all be blessed for their actions today and in the future. The drums sounded and Thomas only then noticed a line of drummers set up along the back wall. They played softly as background to Nan'yehi's song.

The song died down and Nan'yehi turned to the bench in the middle of the room on which stood a large vase. It was one Nan'yehi had made herself, Thomas felt sure.

One of her daughters-in-law came forward from one side of the house with another smaller vase and held it in front of Nan'yehi as she poured the dark liquid from one vessel to another. A second daughter-in-law came from the other side and held a second vessel as she poured the potion into it. Another came forward and held a third vessel and more of the drink was poured into it.

The women moved to opposite sides of the room, while one woman held her vase as she stood in the middle of the front of the room, next to Nan'yehi.

Again, Nan'yehi raised her arms and began to sing. Again, the drummers played, softly at first, but ever louder until the last notes seemed to make the earth underneath their feet vibrate. One final loud beat on the largest drum sounded, then silence held sway.

One of the two young women offered a gourd dipper to their honored guest, Col. Thomas. He took the dipper and scooped up some of the liquid in the vase and drank. Next, the dipper as offered to Tsali. He also accepted the dipper and took a drink from the vase. The women went to each of those sitting on the front bench first, then passed the dipper and the vase down each bench until all present had taken a drink.

At the front of the room, her daughter-in-law moved in front of Nan'yehi and the older women standing with her, offering the dipper and vase to each one of the women, who also took a drink from the vase.

It was unusual for all the women to attend such a ceremony and to partake of the Dark Drink. Those who had the designation Beloved Woman were usually the only exception. However, Nan'yehi insisted this was an important moment in the history of their people and as such, the women deserved to have a seat at this council and to participate fully. Tsali and the other leaders had agreed.

Tsali stood and faced the crowd. "My beloved people," he said, his arms opened wide in an embrace of them.

"Our brother, Col. Thomas brings us news of the response of General Scott to arrangements we have made and given our agreement to. Let us listen as he tells us of his talks with Unaka Scott."

Thomas stood and thanked Tsali, then began.

"I bring greetings from Unaka Scott. He is pleased to be able to tell you that he agrees to allow all Cherokee who have not yet been removed from the Smoky Mountains be allowed to stay. In exchange, he asks that Tsali, his sons and brother-in-law all turn themselves in. They will be executed for their part in the killings of the soldiers."

Thomas paused and looked around the room. This last part of his news hit them hard, he could tell, although no sound or movement betrayed their feelings.

"My dear friend, Tsali, has agreed to give himself and his family members up to Utsala of Oconoluftee. Utsala has agreed that he and his group will accept this mission of execution so that his clan and ours can remain safely in these mountains." Tsali stood as Thomas sat down.

"My beloved family. I know this is a difficult time for us all, but it will lead to one of the most joyful of all times because it will mean our families and our families' families will remain on these lands, from now until forevermore. It is fitting that we bear the sacrifice that must be made. Be joyful and celebrate, my people.

"I go now with Unaka Thomas. My sons will go to Forney Creek where they will be met by part of Utsala's band. No one else is to leave this place until Unaka Thomas returns with word that it has been done and all can return to their homes."

With that, Tsali turned to Nan'yehi and embraced her. They stood for a moment together. It was to be the last time they would be in each other's arms. Nan'yehi tightened her grip as the realization came into her heart. How could she let this man go?

"It is well, my love," Tsali whispered to her, "we will meet again on the shore of the magic lake in the mountains and then I will never leave you. Until then, I will be with you in spirit, in the quiet times." He held her for a moment longer, then held her at arm's length.

"You are my heart," he said, then turned and walked down the center of the Council House and through the doorway out into the night of the Smokies.

The drums sounded, softly at first, then louder until they shook the earth beneath their feet. The people all stood and began to chant, following the lead of the drummers, soft then loud, then soft again, until the sounds of drums and voices died away.

Nan'yehi faced the group. "It is time, my people, to go to your quarters. We must wait until we have word…until we hear…," Nan'yehi stumbled, paused, then continued, "until we hear from Col. Thomas that all has been accomplished." Her voice broke. She paused, then went on. "We will then be able to go home again."

Nan'yehi passed through the crowd of people and walked out of the Council House. Several of the women walked with her, then everyone went to their own quarters. They would mourn Tsali and his sons when the news of their death came to them. Then they would leave for their homes. It would be a sad homecoming for a time. But they would rejoice when spring came and the first green shoots of corn showed their faces.

The sons of Tsali rode to Forney Creek and met with some of Utsala's men. They dismounted and greeted one another. White Feather was in charge of the group and spoke to Alonzo, Jake and George.

"Sons of Tsali, it is a great thing you do, a great sacrifice you make for your families and for your people," he said. "We honor you for your deed this day and for all days to come."

"And we honor you," George said. He and his brothers dismounted and walked to the three trees by the side of the road. They stood in front of the trees, facing White Feather and his men. White Feather tied a white bandana around each man's head. "It is so we will know where to shoot," White Feather said.

The three men stood quietly, their backs to the trees, as they were tied to the trees.
"Our brothers, we pray you hold your rifles steady and fire true," George said.

White Feather nodded. He and his men stood in a line about 10 feet in front of them and made ready to fire.

"Ready," White Feather called. He looked at each of the men in front of the trees. Then he turned to the line of his men and raised one arm, then dropped it.

"Fire!" he yelled. Each man fired a single shot. Those tied to the trees slumped against the ropes that held them. White Feather walked to them to see if they were breathing. He looked back at his men.

"You aimed true, my brothers," he said. "They are on their way to the Great Spirit."

The other men came forward. They began to remove the men from the trees and wrapped them in buckskin blankets, then placed them in their a single grave, along with some vases and bowls filled with tobacco, shells and herbs.

Tsali and Col. Thomas rode out of the mountains together and met Utsala and his men on the bank of the Tuckaseegee River near Bryson City.

"Utsala, you and your men deserve the highest praise from our clans," Tsali said, upon meeting him. "You are going to make it possible for not just your own families but all those Cherokee still in these mountains to remain. It is a great thing you do and I praise you for it. Have you selected a site?" Tsali asked.

Utsala led him to a grove of trees near the bank of the river. They selected one and Tsali stood with his back to the tree. Utsala tied a white bandana around Tsali's forehead. "May your journey be swift and peaceful," he said to Tsali.

He walked back to his men and signaled them to raise their rifles and sighted toward Tsali.

"Ready!" he shouted, then "fire!"

A sound like thunder echoed through the hills from the guns. Tsali was dead. The Cherokee were free to stay in their homeland.

Later, Nan'yehi went to the farm of Burton Welch near Bryson City, N.C., where Tsali was buried. She was taken to the grave and knelt there to mourn her husband. She piled sand on top of the grave with her hands until it formed a mound. She cried as she rocked herself to and fro. This is the last mention found of Nan'yehi.

Mrs. Welch said she saw Tsali shot when she was a child.

"He had a white cloth tied around his forehead," she said, "and it was stained red before I heard the sound of the firing squad's guns." Sometime after that, Mrs. Burton went to Tsali's cabin. "The little cabin looked so deserted with its door open," she said, "Old Nancy's spinning wheel, her loom and warping bars were still there. Outside Charley's plough, stock and harness were there, with the traces of the harness made of hickory bark."

Those who stayed hidden in the mountains and survived eventually formed the Eastern Band of the Cherokee Nation, but they were a tribe without lands. In the 1860s, Colonel William H. Thomas was commissioned to buy land on behalf of the Cherokee since they were prohibited from owning property themselves. Thomas had lived with the Cherokee and they adopted him. He led a group of Cherokee during the Civil War as part of the Confederate Army and participated in the

Battle of Gatlinburg, the only Civil War battle in that town. Later, the lands bought for them by Thomas helped form Qualla Reservation in Western North Carolina.

Five graves lie across top of a steep hill in Deep Creek, NC, hidden from the pathway below. The shadows of the trees fall east-to-west which shows that the graves are aligned north-to-south rather than east-to-west. Cherokee were buried facing north because they thought God dwelled in that part of the sky. European settlers were usually buried facing east so they would see Jesus as He returned. (Photo by Gail Palmer).

Mollie Running Wolfe Sequoyah Cemetery is located just
inside the Straight Fork area of Great Smoky Mountain National
Park on a steep hillside. Many of the headstones are inscribed
in the Cherokee syllabary or writing system for the Cherokee
language, developed by Cherokee Indian scholar Sequoyah
(also known as George Guess or Gist. (Photo by Gail Palmer).

Chapter 7

Deathtrap on the Ridge

It's a quiet place, on top of a low hill, an easy walk through the woods from the road through Roaring Fork, then a short distance up a steep hillside to a level space.

Four markers are spaced evenly across the plateau of the hill with names painted in black on the thin rectangular markers.

Two of those lying here are children of Jasper and Martha Varnell Mellinger, Lenora and Charles. They died during a diphtheria epidemic.

One marker has no name.

The fourth marker has the name Jasper Mellinger. This is his story as pieced together from archival material.

Jasper and his wife, Martha Varnell, lived in a cabin in the area near Sugarlands.

One day in 1903, Jasper left his home and headed out. He was looking for work. He is said to have stopped on his way and stayed with one of the lumber company workers at Elkmont. Later, the man reported Jasper said he was going across the mountains to Hazel Creek to find work. He was a blacksmith by trade.

"Wisht I could find me a job soon," Jasper said. He took another mouthful of smoke into his mouth, held it for a moment, then expelled it through his nose. "Sure enough thank ye for your tobaccee," he said to the man sitting across from him on the porch of a small cabin.

It was about dusk and the road to North Carolina in front of the cabin was empty. The stars were just starting to show in the inky blue-black evening sky.

They sat in silence for a few minutes, taking in the sights and sounds of the evening. From where they sat, they could hear the rush of the river as it ran over boulders and rocks, tumbling down the mountainside toward Gatlinburg.

A whipporwill sounded at the edge of the woods, barely audible under the river noise.

"Well, a man like you orter be able to find somethin' to do if you see the right person. You know, it's a matter of finding the right man to talk to in order to find out what's a-going on," Joe said.

"Yes sir, you're right," Jasper said. He took another draw on his pipe, blowing the smoke up into the air. The stem of the pipe was about a foot long and it was the best pipe he'd ever had. He'd paid Sophie Campbell fifteen cents to make it for him. He held the bowl of the pipe in his fingers, turned it over and knocked it against his hand to catch the spent ashes, then held his hand out over the edge of the porch to drop the ashes from the pipe.

"Well, guess I'd better go to sleep now. Sure do 'preciate your allowing me to stay the night in the barn," Jasper said.

"Why, shore, you're welcome. Let me get you a blanket, might get pretty chilly out there. Just make yourself a bed on top of one of them hay bales or wherever you want," Joe said. He went inside the cabin. When he returned, he held a blanket in one hand and a kerosene lantern in the other.

Jasper took the blanket and slung it over his shoulder. He picked up his long rifle and accepted the lantern.

"Sure enough thank ye," he said.

"Well, now, don't forget to come over in the morning afore you head out. I'll be up and have some coffee and biscuits ready. You'll need to come and eat something with me."

Jasper nodded his thanks and said good night. He held up the lighted lantern and made his way up the well-trod trail leading to the barn. No animals were in the barn, so Jasper stacked some of the hay bales up. He lay down on the top one, then got up. "Reckon that'll do," he said to himself. He laid the blanket down on top of the hay, then blew out the light of the lantern and placed it on the floor next to the hay bales. He touched the side of the lantern and, satisfied it was cool enough, he turned over and pulled the blanket over him.

Next day, he visited with Joe for a few minutes before heading out over the mountains. It was a good day's walk, but he was used to walking.

It was a beautiful day. Jasper noticed the birds singing in the tops of the trees as he moved through the woods. It was as though he were the only person in the mountains. The fog began to lift over the tops of the hills. He moved higher as the sun rose. Now and again, he could see through the trees and out over the whole mountain range.

He could hear the sound of his boots as they crunched into the leaves scattered on the trail. Branches of trees reached out and trailed against his arm or shoulder.

He felt really good, being in the deep woods again. "I'm sorry I had to leave Marthee and the young'uns," he thought. "But I need to find a job so we'll make it this winter. Marthee does the best she can, what with her growing a garden and making our clothes and everything. But I gotta bring in more than a deer once in a while. Here lately, been hard to find enough squirrels to make a mess up or enough rabbits even."

He trudged on up the trail, his thoughts wondering back to Marthee and his family. Up ahead, the trail was rougher, looked like there'd been a rockslide or something, left dirt and branches piled up on the trail.

He slowed down to examine the trail. Looked like he could just step over those branches, or even on some of the stouter logs, in order to make it to the other side. "'Ruther do that than have to go back and then go around. Sure 'nuf add 'bout another day to my trip," he thought.

He stepped forward onto a solid looking branch and it held, didn't bend a bit. He took another step, then another. It was on the fourth step that it happened. His foot went crashing down through a thin layer of branches. A loud snapping sound echoed in Jasper's mind as blinding pain sent him into oblivion.

His body fell off the trail into the underbrush on the hillside. And that's where he stayed, his leg caught in a bear trap that someone had lain across the trail. It did Jasper no good to know that laying a trap on a trail was illegal.

"Oh, lordy," Jasper said out-loud. He started yelling as loud as he could, but eventually lost consciousness. He lay in the woods, off the path but caught in the trap good. He was able to reach into his pocket and pull out part of a biscuit that Joe had given him and nibble on that. He was so thirsty, his mouth so swollen, he couldn't manage to swallow very much of it.

Jasper drifted in and out of consciousness. When conscious, he looked up at the sky, blue at first, then covered with clouds. Dusk began to crowd in over the woods. Jasper slapped at the flies and mosquitoes that came to him. He moved restlessly, testing how tightly he was held. His rifle had been thrown near by. He was able to stretch his arm out until his fingers touched, then grabbed the muzzle. He pulled it close to him and held it to his side. He realized his knife was still in his belt and pulled it out. He held it up and turned it around in the dim light. It looked pretty sharp. He'd used it to skin more animals than he could count. He ran his thumb over the edge, then jerked it back as the edge bit into flesh.

"Oww!," he yelled, shaking his hand to relief the stinging of his thumb. "Maybe I can take this knife out and cut my leg off," he thought. He bent over as he tried to reach his leg where it was caught in the trap. He touched the knifepoint to the skin around the break. Sweat covered his forehead as he held it there and tried to cut into his leg.

"Oh, lord, help me do this," he said out loud. He took a deep breath and pushed the knife through the skin.

He screamed and fell back, unconscious. When he woke, darkness covered the mountains. He looked around, not sure of where he was. He felt the hard ground beneath him. Suddenly, it all came flooding back. His leg was pounding now, nerve endings raw and painful. The knife had dropped to the ground next to his leg. He stretched and tried to reach it, but couldn't. He fell back to the ground.

"Will this never end," he said to himself. He knew now that he probably wasn't going to leave this place. He began to pray.

"Lord, please forgive me for any sins I've committed. You know I've tried to be a good man, but you know I've failed at times, too. Take care of my Marthee and all the little ones. I'm so sorry I won't be comin' back to you."

He wiped his eyes as he began to cry. He hit the ground with doubled fists, rolled his head in desperation and despair.

He lay still for a time, watching the trees overhead. Squirrels jumped from one limb to the other. Birds flew overhead, their wings navigating easily through the tree trunks.

"Wisht I could fly like that…maybe I will soon," he thought, drifting away again into unconsciousness.

After that, he came in and out of consciousness and stayed that way over the next five days, although he lost count. At one time, he thought through the fog of his mind that he heard voices.

"Marthee, Marthee, is'at you? Where are you? Seems like I been waitin' on you a long time," he whispered, then lost consciousness again.

Two men peered through the bushes at him from the edge of the trail. They could just make out the edge of his shoe and they'd heard him talking to himself. It was John Beasly and his son. It was their bear trap that had caught Jasper.

"You reckon he's dead?" the younger one asked.

"Don't know. Guess we'd better get over there and make sure, though. Wouldn't be good for us if he was to make it back and tell folks what happened to him. We'd sure be up for murder, just like that," John answered.

And so, the deed was done. The younger of the two men bashed in Jasper's head and put him out of his misery, then they carried his body away from the trap and down to the river's edge.

"Cut some of them there hemlock branches and cover 'em up," John said. Both set to cutting branches and dragging them to the body until it was well covered. They threw the rifle next to the body and tried to make it look as though Jasper had stumbled and fallen, hitting his head on the river rock.

The older man dusted off his hands and turned to the younger one. "Ya done good, son," he said and clapped him on the back of his coat. They walked down the trail away from the body they'd covered up and left. The younger man twisted his head around to look back, reluctant to leave.

Soon, the sound of their footsteps faded. They left Jasper next to the river. Later bright red, yellow and orange leaves fluttered down, covering the ground and blanketing Jasper underneath the hemlock branches. Snow came and settled over the earth, along with the silence of winter. Spring brought mountain laurel blooms and wildflower covered mountain meadows. Jasper lay peaceful in the mountains for several years, some say five, some seven.

The true story about what happened to Jasper Mellinger will probably never be known. At least two versions are generally pointed out. One version concerns the story told Charles Hall by Zeb Lawson, fireguard in the National Park Service in Gatlinburg. His version pointed the finger to John Beasly and his son. It was the son who was said to have dealt Jasper the actual killing blow at the urging of his father. Then, they took the body and put it on the riverbank and covered it up with broken hemlocks (Hall, Joseph S., 1960, p. 39). The body was on Little River above Elkmont.

However, at some point after this event, the younger Beasly fell ill. He knew he was going to die and wanted to confess his sins. So, on his deathbed, he confessed to killing Jasper Mellinger.

Five-to-seven years had passed since Mellinger died. Jim Cate of Elkmont said he'd talked with the detective who went to the scene of Mellinger's death. Beasly's confession wasn't given any credence, the detective said. For one thing, the wound on the leg was too high to have come from being caught in a bear trap. Also, the fact that Mellinger's killers didn't take the money on the body, a pocket watch and a rifle meant to the detective it was an accident. "John Beasly was too mean a man to leave these behind," the detective explained. The detective said there was no evidence to support the idea that he had been caught in a bear trip. He thought it more likely Jasper had stumbled and fallen, dying from exposure. A coroner's inquest was held there. No true bill was issued by the grand jury and, in this version, no circuit court trial was conducted.

Another version blames Art Huskey and his son as the ones who set the trap, then found Jasper alive on the trail and bashed in his head to keep their bear trap on the trail a secret.

It's not truly known who killed Jasper Mellinger. But if it was the men who'd set the bear trap, they knew the trap they'd set was illegal. It's not known if they used a steel trap or a deadfall. Either way, Jasper was too big a threat to these men for him to live. To them, he was the evidence that they had set an illegal trap.

Rather than save Jasper and take the chance the court would find them innocent because of their good deed, John is said to have told his son to pick up a log and bash in Jasper's head. Or, say some it was Art Huskey and his son who did the same thing. One of them grabbed a stout log, raised it into the air over Jasper and smashed it down on top of Jasper's head. It took only one blow to kill him where he lay. They dug a shallow grave and covered it with brush. The men who killed him left and never looked back, not even to take his rifle, pocket watch or money still in his pocket.

Seven long years passed before someone else found Jasper's remains. It's said they identified him by the pocket watch still in his vest pocket and by his rifle.

In this version, two men were arrested, Art Huskey and his son. They were both tried for the murder of Jasper Mellinger. They were both acquitted when each implicated the other and the jury couldn't decide who was telling the truth.

Later, Art Huskey's son said on his deathbed that he would "see hell today for killing Jasper Mellinger."

However, a Huskey descendent disputes that Art and his son had anything to do with Jasper's murder. They said he fell and wasn't murdered.

Jasper's widow, Martha Barnett, lived in their cabin alone after his death until she became blind and was unable to stay there by herself. She was moved to the Sevier County Poor House. She was such a favorite with the staff there that they bought a coffin for her upon her death with their own money rather than use the pine box provided by the County. Born in 1843, she died about 1952. She was buried in Sevier County burial ground on Lower Middle Creek near Cherokee Mills, a short distance from Sevierville (Russell, 1988, p. 60).

Later, the ridge on which Jasper Mellinger met his death was called Mellinger Death Ridge. It's a spur of Cold Spring Knob (now called Derrick Knob) near Miry Ridge. Derrick Knob was once called Halls Cabin, a rough-built cabin that straddled the state line. Derrick Knob comes from someone by that name who built a cabin near the present day shelter. Later Crede Hall built the herder's cabin and the area became known as Halls Cabin. This cabin still stands at the end of Bone Valley Trail.

It's said at one time, moon shiners ran into the cabin if local officers were chasing them. They could just step over the line into the cabin and the officers couldn't arrest them. A unique feature of the cabin was a hole in the middle of the table that opened through the floor to the area under the floor. They used to throw leftovers into it to feed the dogs underneath.

The Park Service and the U.S.Geological Survey adopted Mellinger Death Ridge as the official name of the ridge, although the name has been shortened to Mellinger's Ridge.

Inscribed marker for Jasper Mellinger.
(Photo by Gail Palmer).

Jasper Mellinger Cemetery where he and his two children are buried. On a hill off the Roaring Fork Road, Herb Clebo said he carried the headstones on his back up to this location. (Photo by Gail Palmer).

Chapter 8

One Drop of Blood

"Ah-a-maz-in' Grace, how sweet the sound,

that saved a wretch like me-e-e-,

I once wa-as lost, but now am found,

Was blind, but now I see…"

The lyrics written by John Newton floated out the church door and spread through the trees and over the mountains, dipping into the hollows and skimming the bubbling waters splashing over the rocks on its way to the valley.

"I love the springtime," Susen thought as she sat on the pew near the back across the aisle from her husband, George Turner. They were attending a special service at the church they belonged to in the community of Meigs Mountain, Missionary Baptist on Jakes Creek Trail. The trail ran in front of the church and was the main connector between two logging communities, Elkmont and Walker Valley, or Tremont as some called it. Meigs Mountain was about mid-way along the trail, and close to Curry Hee Trail which came up the mountain from the railroad line at Little River in Metcalf Bottoms.

Susen, or Sukee as some called her, glanced out the window and saw the mountain laurel leaves sparkling in the sunshine. The church and the cemetery behind it were surrounded by laurel bushes and towering trees. The laurel would bloom in a few weeks. She always loved walkin' along the trails when that happened,

Lots of lovely flowers bloomed all along that trail from spring into August. Even today, wildflowers, mostly trillium of every color, lined the trails. Dogwood blooms were beginning to peek out through the forest in pink and white.

The church was a one-room frame building painted white sitting on a knoll surrounded by mountains. The building also served as a school during the week. Two rows of benches faced the pulpit with an aisle down the middle. Women sat on the left, men on the right. The wall that used to stand in the middle of that aisle to further separate men and women during church services was long gone, but faint markings of where it once stood were still visible to those who looked. However, the custom of men and women sitting apart from one another was still followed, even though the young people sometimes grumbled.

Today was a very special day in the church. It was the day for a foot-washing ceremony and decoration of the small cemetery afterwards. The foot-washing ceremony was held in this church four times a year. Churches in the Smoky Mountains usually met once a month. Preachers served four or five churches and traveled to a different church every week. A foot washing service generally was held on Thursday evening, followed by services again on Good Friday, and then on Easter Sunday. However, some felt the need to hold foot-washing services more often than just at Easter and those services were held on a Sunday. This year, though, the preacher was available only on the Sunday before Easter.

The typical service held during the Easter season followed events in the life of Jesus from the Thursday evening of the Last Supper with the disciples. At that event, the Bible reports that the disciples argued among them as to who was the greatest. Jesus listened, then rose from the table and proceeded to wash the feet of his disciples. Through this act, Jesus showed them an example of how to be a servant to their fellow man just as He was a servant to them by this act and to all by the coming act of His Crucifixion.

The prospect of participating in this solemn and moving service was expected to draw many people whose own church was not scheduled to meet during Easter week. People came from miles around, sometimes so many attended an event such as this that people crowded into the small building and stood along the sidewalls and at the back of the building.

"I hope we'll have enough food for everyone later," Susen thought, looking around the room at the number of people attending. She had cooked for several days as had almost every other woman in the community.

Susen shifted on the hard wooden surface of the pew and smoothed out her skirt, then looked at her brown hand. She thought of the hand of Jesus. Most people in the mountains thought of Jesus as being the same as them, a white man, but Susen had heard people in that part of the world were sometimes brown or black.

"Jest like me," she thought.

"And the nails!" she thought, rubbing one hand over the palm of the other. " How could He have stood the pain!" She shook her head, thinking of the pain.

She sighed, thinking of Jesus and that day. She was glad to be here in the church to remember that day, no matter what color of skin Jesus had.

"And no matter what color I have!" she thought.

"Well, it surly does look like I spend a lot of time outdoors," she thought, "not many people know I'm brown through and through...'cepting George, 'course." She looked at the man sitting across the aisle. He could almost be called handsome. His hair was beginning to come in silver around the edges of the front and sides, and sparkled in the sun just like the laurel leaves.

She put her hand to her mouth, stopping the laughter that almost came. George probab' wouldn't like it if she told him that about his hair. He didn't like anyone to call attention to it. He worked 'most all the time out in the orchards and with the bees and said it was the sun's fault his hair was turnin' silver.

"So far, we've done purty good sellin' apples this year," she thought, her mind wandering. "Honey has done purty well, too. Lots of people have such a sweet tooth they hav' to have a little dab of honey on 'most ever-thin' they eat or drink, 'specially when they gets tired of 'lasses. And now and again, 'course, I kin bring in a little dab of money by a-goin' out to help women when they time comes. 'Course, I'm glad to do it, yes, I am, I always like helpin' women have their babies. And they 'most always give me some little sumthin', them that can, and them that can't, why, that's alright, I'm still glad I kin do somethin' that heps 'em out, 'specially catchin' them babies."

She smiled as she thought of those babies, cleaning 'em up and wrapping 'em in a blanket and handing 'em to the mother. "Oh, the smiles of them mothers when they see that baby," she thought. "And the daddies are no different. They jest light up! It's a wonder to behold!" She hugged herself as she thought about the joy she'd seen in some families. "But, lord, lord, I feel real sorriful for some families, those where the mother already has 10 or 12 young'uns, and them half-fed and bare-foot, even in the winter, sometimes," she thought. She always took along soap and some extra blankets and sheets, even food, just in case the folks didn't have much. Sometimes, she took along a few gowns for newborns that she had made.

"It's the least I can do," she thought.

She looked around at the other women sitting on the same pew and those in front of her and behind. She always wanted to sit in the back because she was so conscious that she was not one of them, even though she was married to George

Turner, who was one of them. No, she was the daughter of a woman who'd been a slave over the mountains in South Carolina. She wasn't the midnight color of some slaves, but a dark brown. Her father had been the white slaveholder, and that meant she was a mulatto. George always liked her color, but some of her neighbors, including those in the church house now, didn't. They especially didn't like what it meant, that she was a Negro.

The singing stopped and the preacher stood up to go behind the pulpit. He placed his Bible on the podium and opened it to the verses he had planned his sermon around. It was said he kept his Bible with him out in the fields and read it on either end when he stopped to rest himself and the horses, then ruminated over it as he plowed the rows, 'til he had it figured out.

He nodded to the men sitting in the pews on either side at the front that faced the podium. It was mostly the deacons and a few visitors who sat there in the "A-men" corner, there to give the preacher support with an "A-men" when they were moved to do so or make some other comment agreeing with what he said.

Preacher Stinnett stood and began to speak. The audience paid close attention to him as he talked.

"As you know, this here's our foot-washing Sunday. Hope you all have clean socks and clean feet." He stopped and smiled, a twinkle in his eyes. "I remember one preacher who spent the night with some of the parishioners. He left his socks inside his shoes beside the bed. During the night, one of the boys put some soot from the wood stove inside his socks. He had quite a surprise when it came his turn to take off his socks for the foot washing," Stinnett said.

People in the congregation chuckled and smiled, shaking their heads. That was a good one to play on a visitin' preacher, they seemed to agree.

Preacher turned to his Bible and began to speak.

"We are here today to join together in remembrance of one of the most solemn experiences in the life of Jesus, the example he set for us to follow and the new commandment he gave us. It's an important example for us all, to be a servant to all, and to love one another.

"Jesus and his disciples were in an upper room havin' their supper. And, you know how it is sometimes, people get to arguing over who are the best loved of someone."

Preacher leaned over the podium as he spoke.

"Can't you just see it? Wahl, Jesus loves me best, one of 'em says. No, he don't! He loves me better. Like a bunch of kids fightin' over who their mama loves best. And we know there ain't no way for a mama to choose one of her children over another." He shook his head. "No sir, can't be done."

"Amen, brother Stinnett," came from the A-men corner. "'At's right, yes siree," one of the women said from the front pew, smiling at the women next to her.

"And 'at's what was happening there in that room that evening," Stinnett said, waving his Bible at the congregation.

"Well," Stinnett said, drawing it out, "Jesus listened for a while then got up and wrapped a towel around his waist...and he took a bowl," the preacher said, his voice rising as he picked up a bowl on a shelf under the podium and held it up for the folks to see, then set it on top of the podium, "and he poured some water into it." He picked up a pitcher of water on the podium and began to pour water in to it.

"Then," Stinnett said, "do you know what he did? It was the durndest thing they'd ever done seed."

Stinnett paused, chuckling at the thought about what Jesus was goin' to do.

"And then, he walked to the nearest disciple, knelt down in front of him, jest as purty as you please. Then, he stretched out his hand and touched that man's foot, and moved that foot into the bowl. He put his hands into the water and cupped some in his hands. Then he poured water over that disciples foot, and used the towel around his waist to dry the feet of the disciple."

Preacher Stinnett paused, then said in a quiet, slow voice. "He touched the foot of that discipline, poured water over it and dried it with his towel. Lord, Lord, what a wonderful thing! Can you jest imagine how wonderful that must 've been, for your Lord and Savior to be ministerin' unto you!"

He shook his head and wiped his eyes with his hankerchief, overcome with the enormity of Jesus' action.

"And then, Jesus went from one disciple to the next washin' their feet as he went, until he came to Simon Peter. But you know what Simon Peter said? He said, 'No, no, Lord, no, it's not right for you to do this for me, I should do it for you.' But Jesus said to Peter, 'Unless I do this to you, you will not belong to me.'

"Simon Peter said, 'Wash all of me, then."

"Wash all of me then, Simon Peter said, wash all of me…'" Preacher said and looked over his glasses at the people sitting in front of him. "Reminds me of that song, 'Wash me in the blood of the Lamb.' Yes sir, that Simon Peter, he was something, he was."

Others sitting on the pews nodded in agreement.

Preacher Stinnett then turned and looked toward the men sitting in the A-men section.

"Now, I'm gonna read from John 13:1-17, where Jesus tells us why he did what he did. 'If I, then, your Lord and Teacher, have washed your feet, you also ought to wash one another's feet. In other words, we're all to be of service, one to another."

"So we're a-gonna' do what Jesus tells us to do. We're a-gonna' wash each other's feet."

"Now, I want each of you sitting in the 'Amen' corner to take off your shoes and socks, then I'll come 'round and wash your feet, just as Jesus did with his disciples. After we get to the end of the row, Deacon Boring, I ask that you'll do me the honor of washin' my feet after I've washed yours."

He walked to the pew and knelt in front of the first man and placed the man's foot into the bowl, cupped some water into his hand and poured it over the man's foot, then dried it with the towel draped on his arm. He proceeded to each man in turn until he reached the end of the pew where he changed places with Deacon Boring. The man knelt in front of the preacher and performed the foot washing for him.

Preacher Stinnett stood and walked to the pulpit.

He looked through his glasses over the Bible at the congregation before him.

"And so, we're all a-gonna do as Jesus did so long ago, just as he commanded we do," he said.

"You've just witnessed myself and the Decons of the Church perform this ceremony.

"Will the rest of you divide into twos, so that each woman will have a woman partner and each man will have a man partner. Decide who is going to wash the feet of the other first, then switch places. That way, everyone will have a chance to have their feet washed and to wash some one else's feet."

Bowls, pitchers of water and towels appeared at the end of the rows at the front of the church, held by female members of the church.

Every one bent to their tasks. Some recited Bible verses as they washed the feet of their fellow parishioner.

"As ye do it to the least of these…" the sound of a woman's voice came over the congregation, while a deeper voice sounded from the men's side of the building "…command that ye love one another…"

The voices rose and fell as each one focused on the task in front of them.

Some of the women, including Susen Turner, removed their bonnets as they approached the pew to begin their part in the washing ceremony.

Susen reached up and undid her hair so that it fell in soft black ringlets around her face and down behind her back to her waist. She took her hair in one hand and pulled it to one side, then knelt in front of the woman sitting beside her, placing the woman's feet one after the other into the bowl of water. She cupped her hands and filled it with water, then poured it over each foot in turn. She bent even closer to the basin and took her hair into her hand to use to dry the woman's feet. Many other women in the room undid their hair and followed the same process.

Preacher Stinnett noted the actions of Susen and the other women.

"Bless you, my children, for you are following the example of Jesus in being of service as well as Mary Madelaine, who used her hair to dry the feet of Jesus."

Several people began to weep and searched for handkerchiefs to dry their eyes.

The ceremony moved down the pews until the time came for one of the women to wash Susen's feet. She had pinned her hair back into place and sat down again on the pew. The women looked up as Nellie Sutton, who was supposed to wash Susen's feet, backed away. She looked at the woman behind her and shook her head vehemently. "No! No, I don't care what they're saying. She shouldn't be here anyways for this, she should be with her own kind!" The woman turned and looked at Susen, her body stiff as she stalked toward the back of the church.

The other women around her looked at one another. One woman, Mistress Whaley stepped forward. "I'll be glad to do it," she said, kneeling in front of Susen, placing a bowl next to Susen's feet. Gently, she lifted first one, then the other, placing them in the bowl, then pouring water over them into the bowl. She took her hair and dried each foot in turn, then looked up at Susen and smiled.

Susen nodded and smiled back. She'd had similar things like this happen to her over the years. People were glad to let her deliver their babies and to eat the food she brought, but weren't willing to do something so much like becoming a servant to a Negra as to wash her feet, not even in church.

Preacher Stinnett had noticed what had happened in the foot washing for the women. He wasn't surprised at Mrs. Sutton's refusing to wash Susen's feet for he knew many resented her being married to a white man. Some in his congregation still held fast to the fact that they'd lost the War Between the States. The fact that slaves had been freed and could participate as members of their society still stung in some groups. They were willing to accept Negras in some roles, but to become a servant to them, even symbolically, was out of the question.

Again, Preacher Stinnet stood at the pulpit. He thought this the perfect time to remind his congregation what Jesus had said at the first foot-washing: "This passage from Philippians 2:5-11 gives us this new commandment from Jesus: 'A new commandment I give to you, that you love one another as I have loved you. This is my new mandate, my new commandment, that you love one another.'"

The women looked at one another as they heard those words, then looked at Nellie to see her reaction. Nellie sat looking at her Bible. Her lips moved as she whispered each word out loud that her fingers traced over so that people close by could hear what she said. She'd found another verse she liked a whole lot better, "Servants heed your masters." It was a verse used as the topic of many a sermon in the Confederate South to slaves during the Civil War and it was a verse she still clung to. "Humrump," she thought, shifting in her seat on the hard wood pew, "these uppidity Negras need to pay more attention to what the Bible really says directly to them and follow it, 'stead of marryin' our white men." She glared at the back of Susen's head. "And she orta' be a-sittin' on that pew in the back, too! Iffen I had my way, that's where she'd be, iffen she's allowed in here a-tall," she thought.

People shifted uncomfortably in their seats and tried to overlook what had just happened. They paid more than usual attention to watching as the bowls of water were being taken away. They didn't want anything to ruin this foot-washing ceremony. It was one of the best ceremonies held at the church.

Preacher Stinnet looked out over his congregation and said: "Jesus concluded the foot washing by looking at his disciples and saying: 'How happy you will be if you put this into practice. How happy you will be if you live a life of service and humility.' We should all remember the words of Jesus and follow them in our own lives." He looked pointedly toward Nellie as she glared back at him.

Preacher Stinnett sighed as placed the towel around his neck. It was a symbol of ordination in the days of the old church. He closed his Bible, stepped back from the pulpit and lowered his head, eyes closed. Sometimes he felt some people would never change. Still, he took heart from the words of Jesus and shared them with those present.

"Let us ask God to forgive our sins and to help us forgive those who sin against us while we are absent, one from another. Amen."

All stood silent for a moment, then turned and walked down the aisle to the outside of the church. They knew they would meet again on Sunday for Easter Sunrise service.

Everyone walked in silence from the church, nodding to one another, smiling slightly, still under the spell of the foot-washing event in which they'd participated. It was a shame Nellie had acted the way she did. That was Nellie, though. She clung to the old ways and old ideas more than most of the people in the congregation.

As they left the church, thoughts of how they might follow the commandment of Jesus to love one another moved through the minds of many. Some climbed into a carriage or wagon to make the journey to their homes or the homes of members of the congregation to spend these few days.

George found Susen and took her hand. He held it as they walked down the path through the laurels toward their home. "I'm so sorry, darlin', I saw what Nellie did," he said. "You know, she and I were a-courtin' some time a-fore we met and fell in love."

Susen squeezed his hand and looked at his face. "Yes, I know," she said.

"Not sayin' that's the only reason she seems to have taken a dis-like to you, but it probly don't help none," he said.

"Yes, I know you're right. But it's a shame she did that. Bless Stella Whaley's heart for steppin' up! She kept Nellie from ruinin' the whole thing," Susen said.

"I know, we'll have to send her and her family somethin' special for Easter," George said.

Susen nodded. They were both quiet until they reached their home, lost in thought about what they had just witnessed, especially the foot-washin' ceremony and what it meant to them.

They walked through the trees to the path that turned toward their cabin. Trilliums of every color dotted the underside of the forest.

Susen sighed. "Everythin' is just so beautiful," she said. She turned to George.

"I love our life together," she said.

He turned to her and squeezed her hand. "I do, too. We are so blessed."

They walked on and soon could see their cabin about midway up a hill, surrounded by deep green fir trees.

"Looks like we got company," George said as he noticed two men on their porch.

"Ummm, wonder who it could be," Susen said.

As they walked closer, they saw one man sitting on the top step, the other in the rocking chair on the porch.

"Howdy, folks!" George said.

Susen smiled and nodded in their direction.

"You George Turner?" one asked as he rose from the chair and walked to the edge of the porch.

"Why, shore 'nuf," George said. He stretched out his hand to shake hands with the stranger standing on his porch.

"Got sumthin' for ya," the man said. He held an envelope to George, who took it and stood turning it over in his hands, wonderin' what it could be. They seldom received mail here at the house, usually picked it up at the post office. And they never had it delivered in person like this.

"That there's a summons, di-rectin' you to come to the courthouse in Maryville to show cause why you shouldn't appear on a charge of breaking the anti-miscegenation laws of the great State of Tennessee," the man standing on the porch said. He was dressed in a suit with a vest and a white shirt with a string tie.

"What's 'anti-miss-ah-gen-nation laws'?" George asked. He still held the unopened envelope in one hand.

"It's when someone white, sech as yourself, marries up with a Negra, such as...," he glanced toward Susen, and ducked his head, his face turning red.

George glanced at Susen, then toward the man on the porch.

"Wal, sure do thankee for yur makin' the trip up here to give me this here thing, but don't rightly know why the State of Tennessee should be interested in what we do up here on this

mountain," George said. "Guess you have to be getting' back
down the mountain."

The man tipped his hat toward George, then toward Susen.

"Well, we've done what we're supposed to do, so guess
we'll head down the mountain," the man on the step stood. He and
the other man moved to the ground.

They looked at one another, and then walked down the trail
toward the road.

Susen glanced at the men as they walked past her without
looking at her and down the trail. She wasn't sure what was in that
envelope, but it shore was takin' holt of George. She knew lots of
people hereabouts didn't agree with them living together, but they
were married and minded their own business, stayin' purty much
out of the way of everybody else and didn't think it mattered.

"Guess I was wrong on that," she thought.

George hurried into the cabin, and then came back out.

"Susen, got to go see Judge Owen in Maryville and got to
go right now," he said.

"You stay here and take care of the critters and I'll be back
soon's I kin...love you," he kissed her on the cheek and headed to
the barn to saddle his horse, then rode down the trail, almost at a
run. It was still daylight, but not by much.

"Think I'll make it before they close," he thought, urging
his horse along. He rode down to Metcalf Bottoms and across
Cove Mountain, then into Tuckaleechee and Walland and after
that, Maryville, the county seat. He pulled up in front of the feed

and livery stable just across the street from the courthouse. He headed across the street. He still might make it, he thought.

He pounded up the wide steps, ran through the columns and pushed open the double-glass doors. He took the steps two at a time to the second floor and opened the door to the office he needed, that of Judge Owen. He paused just inside the door to catch his breath. A young man sat behind a desk and looked at him, then said "May I help you?"

George took another couple of deep breathes, then walked to the desk and stood in front of it. He waved the envelope under his nose, "This here nonsense is what I'm here about. Guess I need to speak to Judge."

"Do you have an appointment?"

"Do I look like I have an appointment? No, I don't, but I expect the Judge will see me. I'm George Turner and two fellers showed up today after church at my cabin in front of my wife and handed this here envelope to me. And I want an explanation."

The eyes of the man behind the desk grew wide and he turned in his chair to face George.

"Oh, you're that fellow," he said. "Just a moment, I'll see if he can meet with you."

He stood and walked into an office at the very end of the floor. In a few minutes, he appeared at the door and motioned for George to go in. George walked past him and stood in front of another desk, this one about twice as big or more than the one in the outside office.

The judge sat in his high-backed chair with his back to George. He was writing on a yellow pad on a long desk behind him. He finished his writing and turned to George.

"Have a seat, young man, have a seat." The judge watched as George pulled the chair out, then sat down on the smooth dark leather. The judge had a white mustache with two long sides that hung an inch below his chin and waved about as he talked.

"Now, what is it you're so hell-fire upset about."

George waved the envelope toward the judge's face. He still hadn't opened it yet, but dropped it on top of the judge's desk.

"This here is what I'm so upset about. The two men who brought it to my cabin today said it was something called 'anti-miss-sin-gen-nation' that said me and Susen can't be married, on account of I'm white and she's a Negra." George took off his hat and ran his hand through his hair. His face was still red from the exertion of riding so hard to get here on time.

"Well, now, George, that's true, there is a law agin people of different races mixing, by being married," Judge said.

"How and when was that brought to your attention?"

"Well, now, let's just say a concerned citizen noticed it and brought it to our attention. You know, we can't let people of different races mix and have mixed children, it just ain't right! Now, you know that."

"Never seems to bother some folks," George said. "Well, what have I got to do to take care of this?"

"You'll have to come to court one day and show us this charge is false, or, if not, we'll have to sentence you to jail for six months and you and your wife can no longer live together."

George sat still for a moment, staring at the Judge. He stood and walked to the window, then turned around and faced Judge Owen.

"So, what you're saying is that the charges will be dropped if I can show they're false," George said, pointing his finger at the Judge.

"Well, yes, that's right," Judge Owen said. "But the only way you can prove them false is to show you're a Negra, too, or to show your wife to be white. And I doubt there's any way to do that, sir."

George looked down at the floor, then up at the Judge.

"When do I have to do this?"

"I kin set a date right now, if want me to," Owen said, reaching for his calendar.

George nodded.

"How 'bout next Monday, the Monday after Easter?"

"That's fine. The sooner we get shed of this nonsense, the better," George said. He put his hat back on, tipped it toward the Judge, then turned and strode out the door. He was in a hurry to get back to Susen so they could figure out what they could do.

It was dark by the time he arrived home. He put the horse in the barn, wiped it down and gave it some water and feed, then went to the house.

Susen opened the door when she heard him on the stairs to the porch.

George held her for a moment, then walked on into the cabin.

"Do you want some tea, George?" she asked.

"Yes, that sounds good, sweetheart. I'll go freshen up, while you're fixin' that."

George went to the back porch and washed his face and hands. By the time he'd finished and went back into the cabin, Susen had a cup of tea sittin' on the table by his chair. She sat in the rocker next to him. They both took a sip of tea and sat looking at the fire in the fireplace.

Susen was anxious to know what was goin' on, but held back, not askin' any questions.

George sighed and turned to Susen as he placed his cup on the table.

"Well, darlin', you know how some people have always not liked the fact that you and I are married."

She nodded, her eyes big and brown, reflecting the firelight.

"Well, somebody's not liked it enuf' to go to the Judge about it, Judge Owen, and they're charging us with what they call 'anti-mis-sin-gen-nation.' Anyway, I'll have to go to jail for six

months and we won't be able to live as man and wife any more…unless I can prove I'm a Negra, too, or you can prove you're white."

Susen's eyes widened even more as she listened.

"How're we gonna' do that, George? It can't be done!" Susen's eyes filled with tears that fell down the side of her face.

"Now, now, honey, we'll figure out sumthin', even if we have to leave this place."

"After all we've done to this place, we'll jest up and leave? Why, that's what somebody wants us to do, can't you see, George? They're just a-sitting by 'til the Judge puts you in jail, then they can throw me offen the land and they can take it for themselves, all the orchards and the fields, everythin'!"

"There, there, Suke, it's gonna be OK. As I said, we'll leave before we let that happen."

George reached across the table and took her brown hand in his white one. He turned her hand over and held it in his. He traced the lines in her palm, then to her wrist. He held his hand next to hers, one white and one brown.

He looked up at her and he began to smile.

"You know what, darlin'? I think I may have just figured out a way to do this!"

He started talkin' to her, explainin' what he had in mind. They'd go to court next Monday after Easter and by golly, they'd prove they were meant to be together!

The rest of the weekend flew by, what with attending Easter services and taking all the food Susen had prepared to share with the people at the Church during the dinner on the ground after the services. People always liked the food she cooked, especially her specialty, apple stack cake. She had baked two for this occasion and it was a good thing, too, because the first one disappeared almost as soon as she placed it on the table.

That night, George and Susen readied themselves for their appearance in court the next morning. They rose with the dawn and rode to town in their carriage and left it at the livery stable as they walked to the courthouse.

They went up the stairs to Judge Owens' room and walked inside. The Judge was there and two men sitting behind the Judge's conference table with him. They were both attorneys in town. Judge Owens introduced them to the attorneys and asked George and Susen to sit at the desk in front of them.

"I'm very sorry that things have come to this, but the law is the law, and we have to make sure people obey it," Judge Owens said.

"Mr. and Mrs. Turner, are you ready to proceed?" he asked.

George nodded.

"And, gentlemen, are you ready?"

They nodded their heads.

George stood and began to speak.

"As I understood this here law we're accused of breaking, anti mis-sin-gen-nation, we're here because I'm white and Susen is a Negra."

He paused and looked at the Judge and the two other men. All three nodded their agreement.

"So, in order for me to be 'not guilty' of this crime, I have to prove that I'm a Negra and not white, or that Susen is white and not a Negra. Do I have that right?" Again, George looked at each of the three men sitting behind the desk. They all nodded.

"Now see here, George, I don't know where you're goin' with this, but we need to move along. I've got other cases a-pilin' up."

George smiled and nodded.

"With your permission, then…," George pulled out his pocketknife and turned toward Susen.

"Now, George, wait a minute! What are you doin' with that there knife?" Judge Owen said. He pushed his chair back and stood up, holding his hand out toward George.

"Why, I'm a-gonna' show you gentlemen that I'm a Negra."

He put the knife on the desk, then turned to Susen, took her right hand, turned it palm side up and gently laid it on top of a hanker chief he had placed on the desk.

He rolled up his sleeve and held his left arm out over the desk, then quickly ran the pocketknife blade over his wrist. He turned and did the same thing to Susen's wrist, then lifted her arm and turned it so the cut on her wrist covered the cut on his wrist.

"What in tarnation do you think you're a-doin'? Judge Owen shouted, his mustache moving with each word.

"It's true if a person has one drop of Negra blood in 'im, it means that person is a Negra, ain't that right, Judge?"

Judge Owen nodded, still standing and staring at the blood now drippling from Susen's wrist to mingle with the blood on George's wrist to the hanker chief down to the top of his desk.

"Well, I'd say I that there blood comin' out of Susen's wrist into the cut on my wrist, why, that gives me more than one drop of Negra blood and that means I'm a Negra, too, now don't it!"

George looked at the three men now standing on the other side of Judge Owen's desk in front of him.

The three men looked at George and at the brown wrist covering the white one with blood going from one to the other.

"Why, Jim, I believe the man has a point," one of the attorneys said to Judge Owen. The man smiled at George.

"I do believe he now meets the definition of being a Negra!" the other man said. He smiled at George, then at the Judge.

Judge Owen looked at both attorneys. "Looks like we have reached a consensus, gentlemen. I hereby declare all charges of anti-miscengenation to be dropped against George Turner and Susen Turner on account of both these individuals meet the parameters set forth in the law for being a Negra, that is, they both have one or more drops of Negra blood in them."

George wrapped a hanker chief around his wrist and Susen wrapped one around hers.

Judge Owen picked up his gavel and banged it on the top of his desk.

He came around to the front of the desk and held his hand out, first to George, and then to Susen.

"Congratulations! I'm glad this case has been resolved in such a sensible way," he said.

The other two attorneys smiled and shook hands with both George and Susen and slapped George on the back.

"It's a good day when we can keep a man out of jail."

"And it's a good day when we can do something good for somebody," Judge Owen said. "Maybe one day, the laws will reflect what Jesus said we should do, 'love our neighbors as ourselves.' "

"Amen, brother, amen," one of the attorneys said.

George and Susen left the courthouse and rode back to their home in the mountains. The next time the census came 'round, they marked themselves as both being "black." In a later census, they were marked as "mullato."

George Washington Turner is listed as "white" in the 1880 U. S. Federal census, while Suke or Susen Turner and their children are listed as black. In the 1890 census, George, Susen and all members of their family are listed as "black" in the U. S. Federal Census for the 6th District of Sevier County.

George was born August 18, 1822, in Tennessee and Suke or Susen was born May, 1842, also in Tennessee. She died June of 1912.

They had six children, two of whom died. Suke (Margaret J.) is the first grave seen when entering Meigs Mountain Cemetery. There are said to be 22 graves here so George Turner may also be among those buried there.

Lem Ownby, longtime resident of Jakes Creek, told this story about George Turner and his wife in a recorded interview. This story is based on that fact. However, it seems some credence is added to the story by the listings in the U. S. Federal Census for 1880 and 1890 and 1900. If the story is true, this event probably happened sometime between the 1880 and 1890 census. No court records have yet been found about this or any similar event.

Below is a copy of the summary in the 1880 and 1900 Federal U. S. Census for Sevier County, Tennessee (Ancestry.com) for George W. Turner and his family. Following that is a copy of each of the census pages represented in the summaries.

1880 U. S. Federal Census, Sevier County, Tennessee

Age:	53
Birth Year:	abt 1827
Birthplace:	South Carolina
Home in 1880:	Wears Valley, Sevier, Tennessee
Race:	White
Gender:	Male
Relation to Head of House:	Self (Head)
Marital Status:	Married
Spouse's Name:	Margarett J. Turnner
Father's Birthplace:	South Carolina
Mother's Birthplace:	South Carolina
Neighbors:	View others on page
Occupation:	Farmer

	Name	Age
	Geo. W. Turnner	53
	Margarett J. Turnner	35
Household Members:	John Turnner	17
	Christopher Turnner	15
	James L. Turnner	9
	George W. Turnner	1

1900 U. S. Federal Census – Sevier County, Tennessee

Name:	George W Turner
Age:	77
Birth Date:	Aug 1822
Birthplace:	South Carolina
Home in 1900:	Civil District 6, Sevier, Tennessee
Race:	Black
Gender:	Male
Relation to Head of House:	Head
Marital Status:	Married
Spouse's Name:	Susen Turner
Marriage Year:	1860
Years Married:	40
Father's Birthplace:	South Carolina
Mother's Birthplace:	South Carolina
Occupation:	View on Image
Neighbors:	View others on page

Name	Age
George W Turner	77
Susen Turner	57
John Turner	38
George H Turner	21

Household Members:

1880 U. S. Federal Census – Sevier County
(section of census page that lists George Turner as "w" or white)

		—	Rachel		W	F	49	Mother			No Occupation
206	207	Turner Geo. W.		W	M	53			1	Farmer
	—	Margaret	B	F	35	Wife		1	Keeping House
	—	John	W	M	17	Son		1	Farm Laborer
	—	Christopher	W	M	15	Son		1	Farm Laborer
	—	James L.	W	M	9	Son			
	—	George W.	W	M	1	Son			

Shown is the trail to Meigs Mountain Cemetery as seen at
its entrance on Meigs Mountain Trail near the intersection with
Curry Mountain Trail from Metcalf Bottoms. Margaret J. "Susen
or Suky" Turner is the first grave on the right.
(Photo by Gail Palmer.)

Chapter 9

Twilight Stalkers

Samuel "Long Hair" Burchfield was arrested in June of 1899 (one source says June 10, another June 18), for the murder of Little George Powell in December of 1897 in Chestnut Flats. George was the son of William Isaac Powell and Nancy Ann Ditmore and was a nephew of George W. Powell Sr., also of Chestnut Flats. Reported in The Maryville Times.

Burchfield was a well-known moon-shiner in the area and looked the part so much he was asked to participate in the Appalachian Exposition in Knoxville in 1910. He set up a still and talked about his experiences, even telling people how to make their own whiskey. He was featured in a postcard advertising the Exposition in which he was shown sitting on a porch, his James Bean rifle across his knees, his dog lying in front of him.

Hale Hughes, 89, son-in-law of Burchfield and his nephew, 16-year-old Ezekiel Hughes, had already been tried for the killing of George Powell Jr. Ezekiel was Burchfield's grandson, the son of Hale's daughter, Dolly. Hale Hughes was sentenced to three-to-20 years in the state prison after he pleaded guilty to the second-degree murder of George Powell Jr. Ezekiel Hughes was acquitted.

At some point after Hale's conviction, he wrote a letter from prison accusing Burchfield of being the one who actually killed Powell. Hughes confessed that he and Burchfield had agreed to try to kill Powell. As competitors in the whiskey-making business, they had a grudge against Powell because he was a witness against Hughes when he was accused of having a still. Burchfield may also have held a grudge against him because of a lawsuit Burchfield lost. In that lawsuit concerning land, the court ordered Burchfield to pay Powell a sum of money and he had to sell just about everything he had in order not to lose the land involved in the lawsuit.

Whatever the reason and whatever their grievances against George Powell Jr., they laid their plans to do away with Powell, their biggest competitor. Hughes was in one place while Burchfield was in another. They were both close to Powell's home, lying in wait. As luck would have it, Powell passed by Burchfield's stand, and he was the one who shot Powell.

However, even though Burchfield was accused and arrested, it's unclear if he ever went to trial. According to Ed Myers, "Cades Cove and Chestnut Flats," Burchfield was indicted on Federal charges by the Internal Revenue a few years later. Myers said he thinks the murder charge must have been dropped in exchange for his being tried on revenue charges. He was never convicted of Powell's murder.

Burchfield is buried in Primitive Baptist Church cemetery in Cades Cove, while Powell is buried in Calderwood Cemetery off U.S. Highway 129. The graves of Hale and Ezekiel Hughes haven't been located.

Burchfield twirled his beard between two fingers, and stroked his long flowing, curly facial hair. He stopped to look around the woods and listen. He'd lived in the woods all his life, so he was in his element, comfortable with his surroundings. He lifted his rifle, made by James Bean, and held it close to his chest, cradling it against him, the barrel pointing toward the blue sky of the cold December afternoon. The day was moving quickly toward dusk.

He thought about the job he had to do today. He'd sworn George Powell would be dead today before sundown and he aimed to make sure that happened. He began walking again, watching the trail as he placed each foot moving along at a steady pace, gliding silently like the shadowy mist rising from the hollows of the hills that surrounded him.

Hale Hughes and Ezekiel were on the other side of the hollow where George's home stood. They were moving toward their stand next to the path George was known to take home.

They weren't certain where he'd be, at home, at one of his stills or returning from Maryville or Cades Cove.

"Either way, it's far sartain he'll meet death today," Burchfield thought.

Burchfield smiled at the thought. It would serve him right, damn George Powell, damn him to Hell. He had no business stepping up to testify against him for having a still when it was well-known George had the biggest still operation in the mountains.

He trudged on down the path toward a rock overhang he knew was in sight of the Powell cabin and the path that came to the cabin from down the hill. It would be hard to miss Powell from this vantage point.

A few more minutes passed as the sun edged toward the rim of the hills surrounding the Flats. Burchfield spotted the turnoff that would take him to the overhang he had in mind. He leaned forward as he moved up the path. It curved around a large boulder then ended on top of the overhang. The flattop of the overhang was obscured from the cabin below by a tangle of broad, flat laurel leaves. They would be curled tight with the coming of the cold night, Burchfield knew.

Burchfield reached the top of the overhang. He walked to the straight, tall trunk of a poplar tree in the middle of the flat area. A shortened branch about shoulder high extended from the trunk of the tree. Burchfield sighted over the limb toward the cabin. Satisfied that he could see the yard in front of the cabin, he placed the barrel of the rifle on a knot on the limb, then checked the line of the barrel aimed toward the front yard. He nodded his approval, propped the gun against the tree, reached in his pocket for the small metal flask he always carried in his coat pocket. He screwed the top off and held it to his lips and took a drink. He wiped his mouth as he screwed the top back on the flask.

Ah, he thought, best whiskey there is in these here hills. He looked at the flask thinking about having drawn enough from the run of whiskey he'd made a few months ago for his own use. He smacked his lips and wiped his mouth again, as he placed the flask back inside his coat pocket.

The sound of laughter came floating through the trees. Burchfield looked through the laurel leaves toward the scene down below. Two of Powell's children were in the back yard with their mother, Martha Gregg.

"Your father's almost home," he heard her tell Althea, the four-year-old, her two-year-old sister, Gertrude. She'd soon have to go inside to their one-year-old brother, William. Martha was pregnant and due in February, when a third girl, Georgia, would be born.

Burchfield shook his head. Well, damn, I hadn't expected to see them here, he thought. He almost turned away, but then he heard a male voice floating up to him. It was George on his way home, calling out to his family.

Burchfield placed his rifle on the tree branch and sighted down the barrel, straight at George's chest as he came up the hill toward the cabin. Burchfield took a deep breath, and let it out slowly. He squeezed the trigger and the shot sounded, echoing over the hills and back. He watched as George fell to his knees, then tried to pull himself toward the cabin.

"Oh, my God!" Mrs. Powell shouted. She and the children had just came from back of the cabin to the front yard where her husband lay. "Children help me with your father." Althea and Gertrude ran to her and tried to help. She pulled and tugged at him. Somehow, they managed to drag him to the front porch. They got as far as the door where he lay, across the threshold of the door. She looked anxiously toward the hillside where the shot came from. What if the gunman is still there? What if there are others planning to come in and destroy the still and kill them all?

She pulled the children inside the house and peered over George's body toward the darkening hillside. She was so afraid, she didn't light a fire, afraid the gunman could see them. She wanted to send Althea down the hill to the nearest neighbor to ask for help, but she dared not take the chance the assassin of her husband wasn't lying in wait along the trail somewhere.

She decided to roll George's body away from the door so they could close it. She and the two girls spent a restless night huddled together on the corn-shuck bed on one side of the cabin. As soon as daylight appeared, she lit a fire and sent Althea to find a neighbor who would come and help. She had covered George's body with a quilt the night before when they had pulled him out of the doorway so they could shut the door.

"Who could be so heartless to do such a thing?" she thought to herself. But then, in the next breath, she knew who could do such a thing…many of the other men in the whiskey-making business could and would do such a thing, given the opportunity.

Soon, she heard sounds of someone coming. Fearfully, she looked out the window at the path from down below. She recognized the neighbor they knew from further down the trail. Another man was with him.

"Thank God," she thought, wringing her hands. She opened the door and walked onto the porch, standing next to her dead husband's body as she waited for the men to approach.

Later, she learned from Dr. Martin that her husband was killed by a single blast from a 56-caliber rifle, same as Burchfield's. The bullet had torn into his chest and clawed its way through his body and out the other side. He had lived but a few minutes after first feeling its impact.

He was killed, they told her, by someone lying in wait on the hillside at the top of a rock outcropping. They'd found a shell from the rifle and a single footprint, size 11.

It hadn't taken long for them to learn that Hale Hughes and Ezekiel had gone to the Powell's with the idea of killing George that day. They were both arrested and tried. Hale was found guilty of first-degree murder but changed his plea to guilty of second-degree murder. His plea was accepted and on May 25, 1898, he was sentenced to the state penitentiary in

Nashville to serve a three-to-20 year sentence at hard labor. Ezekiel was acquitted.

The man Hale Hughes accused of killing Powell was his father-in-law and whiskey-making partner, Samuel Long Hair Burchfield. Burchfield was arrested June 18, 1899, but never tried.

Burchfield is rumored to have called a friend to come to his bedside when he became ill and knew he was going to die.

"Something's been weighing on my heart, lo these many years," Burchfield said. "Hale was right...I shot George Powell.

"I'm not sorry I killed George, but I've been sorry I killed George when his family was there.

"I can still hear the cries of them little children and their mama when they saw their daddy fall. That sound has haunted me every day all those long years since," he said.

"I've held that secret to myself but now I can't rest for thinking on it. Maybe telling you will give me peace and I can go on to meet my Maker."

Burchfield died the next day, August 7, 1917. He was 77 years old. He was married to Evaline Davis, Jan. 27, 1862. They had 10 children. His daughter, Mary Ann, 19, married Hale Hughes, 76. Several of their children had married others of the Hughes' family.

It's not known if Hale Hughes served his full 20-year sentence. Some say he served the minimum three years. Some say he died not long after he went to prison in 1898, after he wrote the letter accusing Sam of being the killer. He would have been 90 years old had he died in 1898.

Sam Burchfield and W. M. Burchfield were arrested December 19, 1907, and ordered to appear in the District Court of Eastern Tennessee in Knoxville on the second day of March, 1908, for violation of the U.S. Internal Revenue Law. They were to appear before Horace Van Deventer, U.S. Commissioner, in his office in Knoxville.

Deputy Collector J. S. Remines testified that he went to Painter Creek in Blount County and found a distillery ready for operation.

"It was still two-thirds full of singlings. I was informed that the land on which the distillery was located was rented by these defendants," Remines said.

"The still was about 500 yards from defendant's house with a well defined path from the house to the still, which was in the woods with a shed over it. There were seven fermenters, one flake stand, set up for operation with about 25 bushels of mash on hand. It seemed complete with all the tools necessary to operate..."

Remines said he didn't see the defendants at the still but at their home.

"William Burchfield was doing nothing, was in the yard, and Sam Burchfield was practicing shooting with his Winchester."

"They went with us to the still after we got there, Oct. 30. We went to the still...defendants denied having any knowledge of who used the still or the still being there or who worked it."

The still was located on Painter Creek with a big hill on each side and no other paths leading to the mill, except the one leading from the house to the mill and continuing to the still...nearest house was about four miles.

Blount County Deputy Sheriff J. M. Brewer went to the still with Remines. He said the still was about 500 yards from the defendents' house.

"It was a grain still, a medium-sized still," he said.

Millard Cupp also went on the raid with Remaines and Brewer.

"At the still we found where bark had been trimmed off trees to make a spout to run from the branch down to the still."

William Burchfield testified that he was a doctor and worked with the railroad company. He said Sam had been sick, unable to work, about the first of August and was sick for two months.

"I used the path to the mill and knew it went by the mill and saw the path beyond the mill used by Noah Williams...who used the path as often as twice a week, carrying a bushel and a half at a time. I was there last spring and Noah was there, said he didn't have any liquor."

Sam was found guilty of not paying income taxes on revenue earned from his still operation. He was fined $250.

A true bill for indictment for illicit distilling was found March 8, 1908.

Then in 1915, Sam was brought up on Revenue charges again. This time, he was also found guilty and sentenced to five months in the Knox County jail, plus a fine of $100.

Sam served two months, then was released on a $300 bond to visit one of his children, who was sick. Later, the court extended his release until Aug. 15, 1916. When Sam didn't show up, a warrant was issued for his arrest. Sam had gone to Robbinsville, N.C., when the officer went to pick him up.

On May 27, 1918, the U. S. Government sent notice to the Knox County Sheriff to pick up Sam in order to finish serving three months and three days of his sentence, plus pay a fine of $100.

It was nine months too late. Sam died Aug. 7, 1917.

Marker in Cades Cove Primitive Baptist Church Cemetery for Samuel "Long Hair" Burchfield of Chestnut Flats community, Parsons Branch Road. (Photo by Gail Palmer).

Samuel "Long Hair" Burchfield and his wife, Amanda. (Courtesy, NPS).

Samuel "Long Hair" Burchfield is shown in a photo used on a postcard to advertise the 1910 Exhibition. He set up a still and showed people how to make whiskey. (Courtesy, NPS).

"Little" George Powell Jr., ambushed by Sam "Long Hair" Burchfield and Hale Hughes.

Martha Gregg Powell, wife of "Little" George Powell Jr. (Courtesy, NPS).

Chapter 10

Devil Child of TwentyMile

This story is based on facts, as we know them, but beyond that is a fictional account of thoughts and actions to help portray reported events.

Sarah placed her hand on her stomach. She was almost nine months pregnant. Most people thought she was carrying the baby high and predicted that meant it was a boy. Others swore it would be a girl.

"Don't matter none to me," Sarah said whenever someone brought it up. "Just so long's it's healthy," she said.

Oh, Lord, please let this baby be healthy, she silently prayed.

Her parents, especially her mother, thought Sarah's baby was the Devil's spawn and told her so every chance they got. If something turned out to be wrong with the baby, her mother thought that would just prove she was right.

"Mark my words, missy, the Lord's vengeance is gonna' come down on your head for your lettin' this happen.

"Everyone thinks it's the Devil's spawn," she shouted. "And you're the one brought it to us. Don't you deny it! God knows what happened, how you consorted with that gigolo, drinkin' and dancin' and fornicatin'," Catherine said. "Preacher done told me that's gonna take you straight to the fires of hell and us, too. We can't even hold our heads up when we go to church, everybody knows what you done and who you done it with…your own first cousin." Her mother hissed that last part, as though she dare not say it aloud for fear of being struck dead on the spot.

Sarah heard her still muttering as she walked down the path away from the cabin toward the river and from Sarah.

Sarah sighed in relief. She loved her mother, but she couldn't hardly take no more of her carrying on so about the baby. She had always wanted a baby, so it seemed to her as if it was God's gift, not something that had anything to do with the Devil. Besides, she had loved her cousin. He was such fun to be with, loved to dance and everybody liked him, too, not just her. She wished it had turned out different. They had talked about being together forever and raisin' a family. Now she didn't know where he was. He'd left in disgrace and she was alone to raise their child. Sometimes it was almost more than she could bear to think about.

"Just gonna have to do whatever I have to so this baby has a chance," she thought.

She knew most of her parents' anxieties were about their friends and family and how that affected the way members of their family and their community looked upon them. After all, her grandparents were Moses and Patience Proctor. They were known for founding the town of Proctor here in North Carolina. Her father, James, was a Civil War veteran who wound up serving on both sides, first with the Confederate forces, then with Union forces when he was captured, and offered a pardon if he would switch sides.

After the war, he and his family moved to Hazel Creek and stayed just long enough for Proctor Creek and Proctor Ridge to be named after him. They then moved to Twenty Mile Creek in North Carolina last year when Sarah learned she was pregnant.

Suddenly, Sarah became aware of a queasy feeling. "Oh, lord, gonna' be sick agin," she thought. She stood up and walked on wobbly legs to the kitchen and found a pan. "I didn't think this mornin' sickness would last this long," she thought. She took the resulting fluids into the bedroom and poured them into the slop jar under the bed. She'd have to empty it later, but couldn't bear to do it just now.

She took the pan back into the kitchen, then walked toward the bedroom, one hand supporting her back, when she felt something wet running down her legs. She looked at the floor beneath her and saw a widening puddle of water spreading out over the floor.

"Mama!" she screamed, "come quick!" She stood still until her mother came runnin' to her.

"What's that Devil Child a-doin' now?" she asked.

"Oh, lord," Catherine could see the water on the floor underneath Sarah. Her water had broken. It wouldn't be long now. She hurried over to Sarah and moved her toward the bedroom, then turned back to the kitchen, grabbed a pan and poured some warm water into it, knelt and swabbed the water up with warm water and soap.

"Go on in to the bedroom and lay down," Catherine shouted. "I'll be in there in a minute. Got to clean up this mess right now."

Sarah grabbed the doorframe and held on as long as she could while she moved toward the bed where she was able to lie down. She wasn't feeling well at all. Everything inside her body seemed to be moving and stretching. It was all she could do to keep from screaming. She was already wet with sweat.

"Well, it's almost time for the birth, if I've counted right," she thought. And there was only one date to count from, so she was sure she knew just when to expect this baby.

Suddenly, she felt another pain. This one felt like a hot poker on her insides. It started in the middle of her stomach then spread, a sharpness and heaviness to it she had never experienced. This pain expanded outward from its center, held its intensity for several minutes, then let go.

Sarah almost screamed, the pain was so intense. She thought it would never end. Afterward, she was drenched in sweat. Her hair lay limply about her face and neck. It was hard to catch her breath. Surely, this can't be happening, she thought. She'd witnessed other women going through childbirth, but didn't remember it being this painful.

"Mama, mama," she cried, her voice weak.

It was several minutes before her mother's face appeared around the door.

"What 'cha want," she said. Then she saw Sarah's face and ran to her. "What's wrong?"

Sarah told her about the pain she'd just had.

"I'd better go get the midwife," she said to Sarah.

"No, don't go, mama," Sarah pleaded.

"I'll ask your Pa to go," she said and hurried out the door and down to the barn.

Soon, she heard the hooves of her father's horse as it clopped onto the road and down along the river toward Tiny Welch's home. She was the midwife best known in these parts, even though she was just barely five feet tall.

Sarah felt better knowing help was coming. Just then her mother came in the door. She carried a cup in her hand and handed it to Sarah.

"Here, drink this, child," her mother said.

Sarah sat up and took a sip. "What is it?" she asked.

"It's catnip tea, it'll help settle your stomach, maybe ease those pains when they come again. Do you think they were contractions?"

Sarah tried to describe the sensations she'd felt, but felt them coming again. She held her mother's hand until they passed. Her mother waited until she'd drank all of the tea, then left her to go into the kitchen to begin boiling water on the wood stove. They always needed lots of clean water when a baby was being born. "Thank goodness I done washed lots of sheets and towels, 'tuther day," Catherine thought. She peeked inside the room where Sarah was lying down again.

"How's it going?" she asked.

"Better, mama, better," Sarah said. She was glad her mother was there and had stopped talking about the baby being such a terrible thing for their family. "I really need your help through this, mama," she said.

Her mother nodded, then turned and went back to the kitchen. There were a lot of things to get ready a-fore the midwife got there. Tiny always brought a lot of her own stuff, she knew, but it would be a good thing to have as much ready as she could.

Things were quiet in the house for a time and Sarah even managed to doze off. She woke, though, when she heard the sounds of people coming in the door. It was her Pa and Tiny. Pa came into the room. He looked at her, his black eyes burning into her own.

"You're goin' suffer for yor sins today, girl. I brung back Tiny and she's the best midwife in these parts, but she ain't a-gonna be able to help you, not for allowin' no Devil child to take life inside you," he hissed.

"Pa, don't say that," Sarah said.

"Well, I'll be right outside the door, but don't be lookin' to me for no hep," he said. He walked toward the door, but turned to look back. "You ain't no daughter o' mine," he shouted.

Tiny came in right behind him and set to work. She looked at him, but knew that people were sometimes excited and acted up during a birth, but all this hub-bub with the Proctors was unusual. She knew they blamed Sarah for getting pregnant and by her own first cousin. And she knew their preacher had talked a hell-fire-and-damnation sermon a few Sundays ago against the Proctor's "Devil Child." It was, in fact, the reason the family had moved to Twenty Mile, nowhere near Moses and Patience Proctor. Jim and Catherine couldn't stand the shame they felt heaped on them by the pastor and by the people of that area of North Carolina.

She shook her head, then walked to the bed and examined Sarah first to see how far along she was.

"Along a-right smart," she said. "You sure you counted up right?" she asked.

Sarah nodded, awed by this small, childlike woman who'd taken over so easily.

"Well, it won't be too long," she said. "Now when the pains come agin, I want you to sit up, if you can, and bend your knees. Sometimes that can ease the pains."

Just then Sarah's father, James, came in carrying a long knife. Sarah's eyes widened when she saw him and she screamed when he bent down over her.

"This here knife is supposed to cut the pain iffen I put it under the bed," he said, holdin' the gleaming steel inches from her face, "but you ain't agonna' get no ease from me, so I'm takin' this here knife outta here." He turned and walked back out the door, his back stiff and unyielding.

Tiny looked at him for a minute. "Well, you never know what people are goin' to do," she said, frowning.

Catherine, Sarah's mom, stood on the opposite side of the bed from Tiny and wiped the sweat from Sarah's face. At least, she was gonna' be by Sarah's side, Tiny thought, even though Catherine's face was grim as she thought about the baby that was being born.

"Weren't right," she thought, thinkin' about the father of the baby and what the preacher had said. She kept her thoughts to herself, though, waitin' to see what would happen. Lord help her, she was hopin' God's hand would reach down and keep that Devil child from bein' born a-tall. She didn't know what she'd do if it come out alive. She knew she couldn't bear the shame, couldn't face her friends and family, couldn't think 'bout takin' it around and showin' it to everyone. "It would be like celebratin' a symbol of the Devil's work right here in our own family," she thought.

Sarah's labor went on for several hours. She sat upright, knees bent and pushed, pulling on the sheet Tiny had tied to both bedposts, her head back. Ear-splitting screams came as she pulled and pushed. All the sheets were soon wet with sweat.

"The baby's doin' good," Tiny said, Sarah didn't see how that could be the case, but she trusted Tiny, so she tried to relax. Still, after another hour, the baby hadn't come.

Tiny examined Sarah and felt the baby. It was ready to come out and was in the right position, but it just wasn't moving along. Tiny reached under her big midwife apron and rummaged around a bit. "Ahh," she said. She held up a small cloth bag and undid the string, then poured some into her palm. "Ta-bak-ee," she said.

"I've used this a-fore in sitc-sea-ations just like this one, so we're agoinn' try it here and see how it works," Tiny said. "Lean back against them pillers and pull yur knees up against yur chest as much as you can and look at me."

Sarah huffed as she did her best to move her swollen body around as Tiny asked.

"I'll do anythin' to get this baby outta' me!" she shouted. She noticed the bag in Tiny's hand.

"What's that?" she asked. Tiny smiled. "Ta-bak-ee," she said.

"Tabakee? What are you doin' with that while I'm being split apart?" Sarah yelled in Tiny's face. Sarah's face was red and sweat poured down her face and dripped from the point of her chin. Catherine held a wet, cool cloth and patted it over Sarah's face.

Tiny sat on the side of the bed facing Sarah and held her palm in front of Sarah. She took a deep breath, then blew so that bits of tobacco flew up into Sarah's nose. Sarah sneezed, once, then again. "Ohhh," she said. "Why'd you do that?"

"Sneezing seems to help move the baby out sometimes when it don't want to come. Looks like it's doin' the job this time, too," Tiny said.

"What's happening?" Sarah asked. A searing pain took over just then and the sound of Sarah's screams could be heard all the way out to the barn, a good 50-feet from the house.

"Glory, glory, the baby's head is out. Just give another big push and it'll come all the way out," Tiny said.

Sarah pushed one more time, groanin' with the effort. Sure enough, the baby came all the way out. Tiny caught it and cleaned it with a damp cloth, reaching a finger into its mouth and clearing it of mucus. She laid the baby on the bed and pulled a length of umbilical cord out from its body. She cut it cleanly in two, holding the part still attached to the baby up while she pulled a long, narrow piece of cloth out of her bag. She wrapped the cloth, called a belly band, around the body of the baby, then pinned it so that it held the umbilical cord in against the belly button.

"There," she said, patting the cloth over the baby's stomach. The bleeding from the cord would stop soon, she knew.

"It's a girl," she said, wrapping the baby in a blanket and holding the bundle out to Sarah.

Sarah held the baby in her arms and looked at its face. "She's beautiful," she whispered. "Look, Tiny, ain't she purty?" Sarah said, holdin' it up so her mother could see it.

"Well, she is that, alright," Tiny said. "Her foot's a little turned and her eyes are too but that usually changes as the baby gets a little older, nothin' to worry about. But I am worried the baby hasn't cried yet."

Tiny took the baby out of the blanket and held it up by its heels. She pulled her other hand back and slapped it against the baby's bottom, once, twice, then a third time.

They all three held their breath as they listened for the sound of new life.

Suddenly the baby gasped, then cried, a good lusty cry. Everyone smiled. A good sign.

The baby's crying brought her father into the room. Sarah held the baby out for him to see. He peered down at the small bundle, then turned on his heel and walked out the door. His first grandchild. And it had to be a Devil Child. Sarah would pay for bringing him a Devil Child as his first and only grandchild. .

"Now, Catherine, get everybody to go on outside while we get Sarah and the baby cleaned up. You know Sarah has to stay in bed for a few days, have to allow all those bones to settle back into the right place," Tiny said.

Sarah looked at Tiny. She was so grateful to this small woman who was so powerful in the birthing room. It gave her confidence she knew what she was doing.

"You're gonna' need to feed this baby in a few minutes, but let me get her cleaned up a bit more. You just lie back and close your eyes for a few minutes, get some rest.

"Catherine?" Tiny called. She had disappeared into the other room. "Different than most first-time grandparents," she thought. "You got some of that catnip tea made? We'll need to give the baby some a-fore she nurses so the hives will come out," Tiny said. "And bring in a pot of that there warm water. We're gonna need to get the after-birth out and then change those sheets."

Tiny turned back to Sarah and took the baby from her and placed it in the crib next to the bed. Tiny put her knee on the bed, then her other leg and crawled up on the bed, close to Sarah.

"Lie back," Tiny said, pushing Sarah's shoulder with one hand and pulling Sarah's night gown up to reveal her still bloody legs and stomach.

"This is gonna' hurt, but we gotta' get that after-birth out."

Sarah lay back. She felt Tiny's hands on either side of her stomach. Suddenly, Tiny pushed down on her swollen stomach. It was still tender from all the pain she'd just gone through giving birth to her daughter. Sarah screamed again.

"Sorry, girl, gonna' have to do it agin," Tiny said. She placed the heels of her palms on either side of Sarah's stomach, down lower.

"I kin feel it in there...it's comin' but gonna' need one more good push!"

Tiny pushed her hands down when she said the word "push." She reached down between Sarah's legs and grasped the end of the umbilical cord and pulled. Water and blood gushed out onto the bed along with the afterbirth sac that had held the baby during the pregnancy.

Tiny covered it with a towel and wrapped it up, then held it out toward Catherine.

"Here, wrap this up some more and give it to Jim. He's agonna' have to bury it deep somewheres away from the cabin so's the animals won't get to it."

Catherine held another towel in her hands and she wrapped the after birth in that towel, too. Blood was already seeping through the first towel and onto the floor.

Catherine nodded and ran out of the room toward the door. She stuck the package outside the door and yelled for Jim.

"Come and take this and bury it deep somewhere's so the dogs nor nothing can dig it up!"

She went into the kitchen and washed her hands before she fixed some tea, then to the bedroom in a few minutes with a cup and a spoon she handed to Tiny, then left again. Soon she was back with a stack of clean linen and a clean gown for Sarah.

Tiny took the spoon and placed a few drops of tea on the baby's mouth. The baby started making suckin' motions so it was easy for her to take in a few drops. She placed the baby in the crib next to the bed and turned to Sarah.

"You got a name for this young'un yet?" she asked as she bent down, rolled Sarah over on one side and began removing the bedclothes from underneath. Catherine put clean sheets on the side Tiny had just removed the others, then they rolled Sarah back over onto the clean side and finished removing the soiled linens. Catherine helped Sarah take off the old gown and put on the clean one.

"Not yet, but thinking about naming her Hope," Sarah said. "My grandmother's name is Patience, so 'Hope' would kinda fit in with that. Plus, I have so much hope in my heart for this child." Sarah smiled up at her mother.

Tiny fluffed the pillows and Sarah leaned back against them. "It feels wonderful being in a clean bed again," she said. "Thanks, Tiny. And, thanks Mama. You've been wonderful. I know you're still not happy about all this, but I don't think I could of made it without your help."

Her mother's features softened for just a moment as she looked at her only child. "Why did things have to be so hard?" she thought. She didn't wanna' go against the preacher's words, but she loved her daughter and didn't want to hurt her either.

"Catherine, bring the baby over here so's we kin go ahead and let her nurse just a bit a-fore Sarah goes to sleep," Tiny said.

Catherine walked to the crib and looked down at the baby. "Such an innocent-looking child," she thought. "How could God be against it? The child didn't have any choice in who its parents were. Please, God, don't make me do something to this baby."

She wrapped the baby in a blanket, then handed it to Sarah. Sarah pulled her gown open and placed the baby against her breast so it could begin nursing. Sarah smiled as she watched her baby feed. "She's a-goin' at it good," she said.

Tiny watched for a minute to see everything was going all right.

"Well, reckon everyone's fine, so I'll head on home," Tiny said. She began cleaning up and packing her bag. She placed a small bag of herbs on the table next to the bed. "Catherine, use these to make a tea for Sarah after the baby's finished nursing. It'll help her get a good long rest and I think she needs one now. Send Jim to come get me if you need any help, you hear?" Tiny said, looking at Catherine.

The two women walked out of the bedroom and into the kitchen. Catherine had a sack of eggs and two jars of honey to give Tiny for her help delivering the baby.

"Why, thank ye," Tiny said, picking up the bags.

Catherine went to the door to the porch. "Jim, can you take Ms. Tiny back home now?"

Jim jumped up on the porch and took the bags from Tiny. "Why, shore I can, come along Ms. Tiny, I've got the horse hooked up to the carriage so we can ride a little more comfortable on the way back."

"Thank ye for being so good with our gurl," Catherine said, touching Tiny on her shoulder.

"You're right welcome," Tiny said. "Remember to give her some of that tea in a few minutes."

Catherine nodded as she watched Tiny and her husband, Jim, ride in the carriage down the road. She stood there a few minutes longer after she lost sight of them. "What am I to do?"

she thought. "Everyone's gone and Sarah's gonna' be asleep soon. It'll just be me and the baby." She shook her head, trying to clear it. The voices she'd noticed right after she knew Sarah was about to give birth had grown louder now and wouldn't go away. "What do you want of me? How can I kill this child of my child, even iffen it is the Devil's spawn?" she cried out to the wilderness around her.

"Mama, are you out there?" Sarah said.

"Yes, child, I'm comin'. Just need to make some of this tea for you. It'll have to set just a few minutes so's it won't be too hot."

She walked into the kitchen and poured some water over the herbs in the sack that Tiny had left. She let them soak in the water for a few minutes, then took the cup in to Sarah.

She picked the baby up and placed her in the crib while Sarah drank the tea.

She couldn't stand to look at the baby. The voices were becoming louder, more insistent now and she knew she'd have no choice but to do as they said. "It'll be easy," they said. "No one's here but you. Jim won't be back for about an hour. Sarah will be asleep. It won't be hard. Take the baby outside! You'll know what to do with this Devil's child!" the voices said. "You don't want this Devil child of your daughter to be let loose on the world, do you? Remember what the preacher said. You and your family will be doomed to the fires of hell if you don't do something."

Catherine shook her head. She couldn't think right now. She watched Sarah as she finished the tea and lay back against her pillow. Her eyes began to flutter and soon she was asleep.

Catherine picked up the cup Sarah had placed on the table and took it into the kitchen. She stood at the sink for some time, then straightened her shoulders, turned and walked into the bedroom to the crib. She looked down at the baby. It was on its back, asleep. She put her hand on its chest, then caressed its head, held its tiny hand in her own, traced its mouth with her finger. Before she realized what she was doing, she had picked the baby up and was carryin' it outside, just like the voices said to do. Its eyes were open and she could see how big and blue they were as she looked up at Catherine, it's mouth still working as though suckling. It reminded her of a baby pig. She began walking faster. She knew what to do now. The voices were urging her on..."do it, do it, do it!" they chanted.

She walked straight to the hog pen. Several piglets were running around among the larger animals. She took one last look at the baby, then raised it above her head and hurled it into the middle of the pen. The baby began to cry and the animals turned toward the sound.

It didn't last long, just a few seconds, really. Catherine sighed with relief. The voices were gone. They had fled on the baby's last breath.

She turned and walked back into the house. She looked at Sarah, who was asleep. She decided to sit in the rocking chair next to Sarah.

"I'm so sorry, my darlin' girl, but I had no choice, I had to get this evil away from us," Catherine whispered as she took her daughter's hand in her own and patted it.

Then she stood and left the room

Her husband discovered the baby was gone when he came back and went into the room to see what this Devil Child looked like. The crib was empty. Sarah was the only one in the room. Her father shook her awake. "Sarah, what's happened to your Devil child?" he asked.

Sarah woke and looked for the baby. She was confused for a few seconds, then realized she was gone. Surely, she hadn't dreamed the whole thing, being pregnant, going through labor, seeing and holding the baby.

She looked up at her father, tears beginning to roll down her cheeks.

"What's happened to my baby?" she asked.

"The Devil probably took it with Him, but I'll look around," her father said. He went into the other room, looking for his wife.

"Where are you, my darlin' baby, my baby Hope, what has happened to you?" she cried. "Come back to me, Hope, please come back," she pleaded. She began sobbing as she realized the baby was nowhere in the house.

"Catherine, where's that Devil Baby? Did you take it outside, is that what happened?" Jim asked his wife.

Catherine shook her head, then a slow smile came over her face.

"You know we're better off with that Devil child dead, don't you?" she whispered.

Jim looked at his wife. He placed his hands on her shoulders and looked into her grey eyes. "You did it, didn't you, woman! By God, you've done it!" Jim said. He couldn't believe it, but as he realized it was true, a slow smile spread over his features. They were free now. Catherine's act settled the matter. They didn't have the curse of this Devil Child a-hangin' over them no more. It was a miracle.

"Thank ye, Lord," he whispered. He jammed his hat down over his forehead so it helped hide his face from view.

"Mama," Sarah said.

They turned around to see Sarah standing in the doorway.

"Did you do this, Mama? Did you take away my baby?" Sarah asked softly.

Her mother stood in the middle of the room and looked back at her daughter.

"Yes," she whispered. "Yes, I took it, and I threw it hard as I could into the hog pen! Didn't take them pigs long to kill it. It was the Lord's will, and I done it because He told me to do it."

Sarah and her father looked at Catherine then at one another. The only sound in the house was the drip of water from the faucet.

"Mama, what are you saying? You can't mean that!" Sarah cried. She held to the doorframe to keep from falling. Her father turned and ran out the room. Sarah heard the sound of his running down to the hog pen. Silence filled the room.

She fell to her knees. She could not bear to think of what had happened to her beautiful baby. Sobs shook her shoulders. Her mother came to her and held her.

"It's alright, baby girl, it's alright," she said to Sarah, stroking her hair, trying to comfort her.

"Mama, don't you know what you did?" Sarah turned to ask her Mother.

"Why, yes, child, I did what the Lord asked, and now we're free, we can hold our heads up when we tell folks what we did to rid ourselves of this demon in our midst," Catherine said.

Her father appeared at the doorway, holding a small bundle in his hands. The bundle was the blue blanket the baby had been wrapped in, torn and tattered now. The blanket and his hands were covered in mud mixed with blood. Sarah recognized the blanket and knew it was true. Her mother had thrown her baby into the hog pen and she was dead. She knew what she had to do now. She turned to her father and began to plead with him.

"Pa, we can't let anyone know Mama did this horrible thing. We have to tell them I rolled over on her and suffocated her and in my grief, I – I – I …oh, it's too horrible to say. Say it was just an accident, I was throwing slops into the pen and was holding Hope in my other arm, but somehow she moved and fell into the pen. I was too weak to pull her out," Sarah said.

Sarah looked up into his face. "You hear me? We have to tell people I'm the one who killed the baby. Please, I can't lose my child and my mother," she pleaded.

Jim nodded slowly. "Not much left now…guess I'd better make a coffin anyway for what's left?" he asked Sarah, his anger spent. He looked smaller to Sarah, deflated somehow.

She nodded, walked to him and took the blanket wrapped around a tiny bundle in her arms. She held it to her as she walked to the rocking chair and sat down. She closed her eyes and began crooning softly.

"Hush, little baby, don't you cry…" she sang, then hummed, rocking to the rhymn of the song.

"Everythin's gonna be all right now," Catherine said.

"Yes, Mama," Sarah said.

On April 6 of 1885, eighteen-year-old Sarah Jane Parton was sentenced to life in prison for killing her newborn daughter. Four years later, someone went to the authorities and revealed the true story and named the person who had really killed the baby. The court reversed its decision, found her not guilty and released her. The family member who is thought to have killed the baby was never brought to justice. It's still not known who killed Sarah's baby, but it's said the fact that its parents were first cousins was a terrible affliction socially for the family. However, the above account is fiction based on facts found in archival records and interviews. Court records have not been found.

After Sarah was released, the family moved to Cades Cove. While there, Sarah married Reuben Maynard. They had no children. However, Sarah had a son, Willie Proctor, with Harry Myers of Cades Cove. Some think Sarah is buried in Lawson Cemetery in Cades Cove, but there is a grave marker for Jane Maynard (1867-1918) in Primitive Baptist Church Cemetery in Cades Cove. Most likely, she used her middle name, Jane, once in Cades Cove, and her mother used Millie rather than Catherine. Sarah Jane is buried alongside her parents, James Proctor (1834-1910) and Millie Welch (1835-1911, and her sister, Gnetty (1878-1955). Also, the father of Willie, her son, Harry Myers, is buried in the same family area. After Sarah died, Reuben married Gnetty. Reuben's gravesite is unknown.

Sarah's baby was buried in an unmarked grave near their cabin in Twenty Mile, NC

Cades Cove Primitive Baptist Church Cemetery, a view of the cemetery and the rear of the church building. Markers for Sarah Proctor Maynard, her husband, parents and sister are located here. (Photo by Gail Palmer).

Marker for Sarah Jane Proctor Maynard. Jane

married Reuben Maynard who married Gnetty, her sister after Jane died. Reuben's burial site has yet to be located. (Photo by Gail Palmer).

James Proctor, TwentyMile, NC (at his tub mill).
(Photos, courtesy, NPS)

Margaret Proctor,wife of James.

This photo is of the Jim Proctor family. However, none of the individuals are identified. It can probably be assumed that "Jim" is second from the left in the front row.

217

Margaret, his wife, may be the woman standing behind him, while the woman seated to Jim's right may be one of his daughters, Gnetty or Sarah. (Courtesy, NPS).

James Proctor marker, Primitive Baptist Church, Cades Cove. James also served in the Union Army when he was offered that choice as a prisoner-of-war. (Photo by Gail Palmer).

Margaret Proctor marker, Primitive Baptist Church, Cades Cove. Wife of James, mother of Sarah Jane Proctor. (Photo by Gail Palmer).

Marker for Gnetty Proctor Maynard is located in Primitive Baptist Church Cemetery off the Loop Road in Cades Cove. (Photo by Gail Palmer).

Reuben Maynard, husband of Sarah Jane Proctor Maynard, Cades Cove. Reuben's grave has yet to be located. (Courtesy, NPS).

Headstone in Proctor Cemetery, parents of James Proctor.

Moses and Patience moved from Cades Cove and became the first settlers in Proctor, NC. (Photo by Gail Palmer).

About the Author

Dr. Gail Palmer has deep roots in East Tennessee and the Smoky Mountains and has developed a love for the people and their stories. Her maternal grandparents, John Marion Sparks and Elizabeth Jane Shuler, both lived in Cades Cove. John was born there, while Elizabeth came from just over the mountain in Dry Valley, Tenn.

Gail's feeling of connection to Cades Cove and the Smokies strengthened over time and fueled her curiosity about the mountains and the people who lived there. By the time she finished her degrees (undergraduate, masters and doctorate) at the University of Tennessee, Knoxville, she knew she could use what she had learned to find out even more about her ancestors and the region. She began to look for ways in which to share what she'd learned about her ancestors and people of the Smokies.

Gail was born in Maryville, Tenn., but attended schools in Dunedin and Clearwater, Fla., when her family moved there and where her parents (James and Mary Palmer) operated a small furniture store. It's slogan: "You furnish the girl, we furnish the home." She worked in various editorial and writing positions in Florida and New York. After moving to Knoxville, she worked in the office of the School of Journalism and finished a bachelor of science and masters in journalism. She served as the first adviser in the College's Advising Center and was eventually appointed director of the Center. She also served as adjunct instructor in journalism and taught basic news writing.

Gail began gathering material for a book on the Smokies soon after finishing her Ph.D. in 1994. She completed this work in 2006. It's scheduled to be published by Great Smoky Mountains Association. Other work has appeared in national and local publications.

In 2009, she wrote and produced a DVD, "Sacred Places of the Smokies," featuring stories about individuals who lived in the Smokies before Great Smoky Mountains National Park was created. Then, in 2010, she wrote and produced a second DVD, "When Mama Was the Doctor: Medicine Women of the Smokies." Both DVDs are available at GRSM Visitors Centers and at venues in Maryville, Knoxville and Townsend, including Southland Bookstore and Hastings Bookstore, as well as amazon.com. Black Bear Café in Townsend is another location in which to find these DVDs and the book described below.

"GSMNP: In the Beginning…Fact, Legend and Eminent Domain," serves as a brief chronicle of events that led to the formation of the Park and the story of inclusion of lands within the area on which individuals and families made their homes over the years. It shows how decisions made by individuals interested in creating a national park came about and the effect they eventually had on the mountain people. This book is available on amazon.com as well as Southland Bookstore and Hastings

Bookstore in Maryville, Tenn., and Black Bear Café in Townsend.

Mary Sparks, Gail's mother, is sitting in the rocker. The children (l. to r.) are Duey, Roy, Dutch, Mary, May Belle and Margie. This photo was probably taken in Santee, Georgia, which is where the family moved to for a short time. The children's father, John Marion Sparks, and their mother, Elizabeth Shular, left Cades Cove in the winter of 1912 and drove a wagon across the mountains into North Carolina and south to Santee, Ga., in search of Catherine Russell, John's mother. They stayed there for a time and visited with Catherine while there, but lost touch with her later. Their daughter, Mary Jane, was born in Santee, GA, in May of 1912. She died in 1997 and is buried in Magnolia Cemetery, Maryville, TN. (Courtesy, Mary Sparks Palmer, deceased).

Sources

Arthur, John Preston. Western Northern Carolina: A History. Raleigh,1914.

Beverley, Robert. The Western North Carolina Almanac and Book of Lists, 2nd ed. Sanctuary Press, Franklin, N. C. 1991. Blackmum, Ora. Western North Carolina: Its Mountains and Its People to 1880. Appalachian Consortium Press, Boone, N.C. 1977.

Brewer, Alberta and Carson. Valley So Wild: A Folk History. East Tennessee Historical Society, Knoxville,Tenn. 1975.

Browder, N.C. The Cherokee Indians and Those Who Came After. Hayesville, N.C., 1973.

Brown, Fred. "Cold Mountain: From Obscurity to Literary Fame: Mountain Communities take Notoriety in Stride." Knoxville News-Sentinel, April 19, 1998, Section E, pages 1 and 3.

Ibid., "Meet the Major: Inman Family History Runs Deep and Wide on Cold Mountain." Knoxville News-Sentinel, April 19, 1998, pages 1 and 2.

Brown, Margaret Lynn. The Wild East: A Biography of the Great Smoky Mountains. University Press of Florida, Gainesville, Fla. 2001.

Bryan, Charles Faulkner. The Civil War in East Tennessee: A Social, Political and Economic Study, Thesis 78b.B689, The University of Tennessee, Knoxville, August, 1978.

Burns, Inez P. History of Blount County, Tennessee, From War Trail to Landing Strip, 1795-1955. Nashville, 1973.

Bush, Florence Copeland. <u>Ocona Lufta Baptist Pioneer Church of the Smokies</u>. Misty Cove Press, Concord, Tenn., 1990.

Ibid., <u>Dorie: Woman of the Mountains</u>. University of Tennessee Press, 1992.

Cades Cove Baptist Church Book, 1827-1905 In possession of Ray Taylor, Maryville, Tenn.

Callahan, North. <u>Smoky Mountain Country</u>. New York, 1952.

Cate, Herma R., and Martha H. Callaway, eds. <u>Back Home in Blount County: An   Illustrated History of Its Communities</u>. Blount County Historical Cherokee County Historical Museum, Murphy, N. C. 1984.

Costner, Ella V. <u>Song of Life in the Smokies</u>. The Brazos Press,Maryville, Tenn. 1971.

Crabtree, Margaret Stinnett. Rememberin' The Little Greenbrier School and Primitive Baptist Church, unpublished.

Crane, Verner W. <u>The Southern Frontier, 1670-1732</u>. Ann Arbor, Mich., 1929.
Trust, 1986.

Creekmore, Betsey Beeler. <u>Knoxville</u>. The University of Tennessee Press, Knoxville. 1958.

Defoe, Don, et al, eds. <u>Hiking Trails of the Smokies</u>. GSMNHA, Gatlinburg, Tenn. 2001.

Dobelis, Inge N., ed., <u>Magic and Medicine of Plants</u>, The Reader's Digest Association, Inc., Pleasantville, NY, 1986.

Dockery, Carl, ed. <u>Marble and Log: The History and Architecture of Cherokee County, N. C.</u>

Dykeman, Wilma, and Jim Stokeley. <u>Highland Homeland: The People of the Great Smokies</u>. NPS History Series, Washington, D.C. 1978.

Edwards, Lawrence. "History of the Baptists of Tennessee with Particular Attention to the Primitive Baptists of East Tennessee." Master's thesis, University of Tennessee, Knoxville, 1941.

Folmsbee, Stanley J., et al. *History of Tennessee*. 2 vols. New York, 1960.

Garrett, William R., and Albert V. Goodpasture. *History of Tennessee*. Nashville, 1903.

Glassie, Henry H. "Southern Mountain Houses: A Study in American Folk Culture." Master's thesis, State Univ. of New York at Oneonta, 1965.

Hart, Roger L. <u>Redeemers, Bourbons & Populists: Tennessee 1870-1896</u>. Baton Rouge, 1975.

Holland, Lance<u>. Fontana: A Pocket History of Appalachia</u>. Appalachian History Series, Robbinsville, N.C. 2001.

Lefler, Hugh T. <u>History of North Carolina</u>. 2 vols. New York, 1956.

Little, Edith Burns, Blount County Cemetery Records, 1980.

National Park Service, Great Smoky Mountains National Park.

Noah 'Bud' Ogle Place: Self-Guiding Trail; Cataloochee Auto Tour, 1976.

Oliver, Elder William Howell, 1857-1940 and Elijah Oliver, 1829-1905, Cades Cove, Tennessee; Chapter II, page 19-35, <u>The Sketches of the Olivers: A Family History</u>, 1726-1966, Col. Hugh R. and Margaret T. Oliver, 1984.

Orr, Horace Eugene. "The Tennessee Churches and Slavery."
Master's thesis,Univ. of Tennessee, Knoxville, 1924.

Shields, A. Randolph. The Cades Cove Story. Gatlinburg,
Tenn., 1977.

_____. The Families of Cades Cove, 1821-1936.
Maryville, Tenn., 1981.

Smoky Mountain Historical Society, In the Shadow of the
Smokies. Sevierville, Tenn. 1993.

West, Carroll Van, ed. The Tennessee Encyclopedia of History
and Culture,Tennessee Historical Society, 1998.

Woodward, Grace Steele. The Cherokees. Norman, 1963.

Other sources such as court case materials:
State of Tennessee Library Archives, Nashville,Tenn.
Federal Library Archives, Atlanta,Ga.

Interview transcripts; digital copies of interviews:
National Park Service Library and Archives, Gatlinburg, Tenn.

Other works by Dr. Gail Palmer

"Sacred Places of the Smokies," DVD
"When Mama Was the Doctor: Medicine Women of the Smokies," DVD

Book - GSMNP: In the Beginning…Fact, Legend & Eminent Domain

Works in progress

Smoky Mountain Tales Book Series
        Vol. 2, More Feuds, Murder & Mayhem

Dr. Gail Palmer
Smoky Mountain Publishers
P.O. Box 684
Alcoa, TN 37701
lpalmer@utk.edu
865-724-4959

This double cantilever barn in Cades Cove near the Tipton Place. depicts the style barn that was the topic of <u>East Tennessee Cantliver Barn</u> by Marian Moffitt and Lawrence Woodhouse, August, 1993. The structure with no supporting posts under the overhang allowed cattle to gather underneath. The opening in the middle allowed farmers to pull their wagons into the center of the barn. (Courtesy, Kathleen Puckett)